HOBO
PASTORS

WISDOM FOR LIFE ON THE ROAD

by

ANDY MCQUITTY & LARRY PARSLEY

Published by Leadership Books, Inc.
Las Vegas, NV – New York, NY
LeadershipBooks.com

ISBN:
978-1-965401-62-0 (Hardcover)
978-1-965401-63-7 (Paperback)
978-1-965401-64-4 (eBook)

LEADERSHIP
Thoughtful, Relevant Leaders From Around The World
BOOKS

TABLE OF CONTENTS

INTRODUCTION

The book you hold in your hand admittedly has an odd title. Let us explain.

In his 1980 book *Knights of the Road*, Roger A. Bruns wrote a history of "hobos": migratory workers who made use of the railways for free transportation. These men (and a few women) had memorable monikers, like Frying Pan Jack, Scoopshovel Scotty and Boston Betty. Some were looking for a job. Others were just looking to see the country. According to Bruns, regardless of their backgrounds, they all "shared a common need: to quench a thirst for moving; to trust their fates to the whimsical notion that a better life lay somewhere down the track."[1] They did a lot of manual labor, the kind of work you might do with a *hoe* (and such were called "hoe boys"). They formed friendships as they rode the rails from job to job, and famously helped each other through often dangerous and destitute situations by leaving hobo "signs".

These symbols, written in chalk or coal, were used to provide directions, information, and warnings to other hobos. Common signs included "turn right here," "beware of hostile railroad police," and "food available here." Every summer, in the town of Britt, Iowa, tourists

---

[1] Roger A. Bruns, *Knights of the Road* (MeHTUEN 1980). 8

gather at a weeklong festival called the National Hobo Convention, where you can peruse authentic hobo artifacts, including a glossary of hobo symbols and their meanings. My favorite is that of a comb with eight teeth, symbolizing the presence of a dog with many teeth!

As odd as it may sound, we veteran pastors resonate with those symbols that one hobo would leave for another. We both admit that while we tried to study hard in seminary, most of what we know about ministry we learned AFTER graduation. We've found unexpected situations to be a wonderful teacher. We have learned, through trial and many errors, the dangerous backyards and cozy porches of modern ministry. And we wish to share with you the signs we discovered on the journey.

Our seminary textbooks, as helpful as they were, did not anticipate the twenty-first century realities of trying to minister in a post-Bible Belt cultural milieu. How do we share the grace and truth of Jesus in a morally chaotic world? As religion declines and spirituality rises, where is a pastor's place in the conversation? One of Larry's pastor friends described getting a call from a distraught family who had just suffered the loss of a dearly loved pet dog. They asked him to say a few words at the dog's burial. None of our minister's manuals feature templates for canine eulogies!

We feel this gap acutely. Both of us benefitted from wise and sincere professors who did their best to prepare us for the tasks they anticipated we would face. But could any of those learned saints have been able to anticipate ministering in a world filled with email and social media, podcasts and video venues, atheist "churches," and weddings whose budgets approach the GDP of some small countries? We were not trained in conducting those funerals where we were asked by the grieving family *"not to mention God because the deceased would not have wanted his service ruined with all that religious hooey."*

To use an aviation metaphor, you might say that seminary was an excellent classroom training for pilots. Pilots will quickly learn, however, that when the wheels actually come up, a whole new leadership curriculum comes at them fast and furious. If we are to survive, we must master this new practical curriculum ASAP and place it alongside our classroom books.

Unfortunately, Andy and I both have friends who didn't walk away from their first landing because they were woefully unschooled in this practical ministry curriculum. They were excellent theologians and eloquent preachers, but they just did not know where the quicksand was. They washed out of ministry because no one had given them a flashlight along with their Master of Divinity degree.

One day over lunch at one of our favorite barbecue spots, we began to daydream about a book for some of the more unexamined chapters of the ministerial life. We agreed that if we were going to write a book for pastors, it would likely not be a coffee table book for Oxford dons. You would more likely find it among the train tracks of the 1930's – a book for Hobo Pastors.

So please think of us as a couple of wizened hobo pastors, leaving signs for our younger ministerial friends. We want to share with those new to the rails how to survive in ministry: where to find the food, who's got the guns, how to avoid the junkyard dog, and where to camp without getting bushwhacked.

If you are in vocational ministry, or are close to someone who is, we thought you might find strength in these time-tested words passed down to those new on the journey. We would love for you to follow along and add your signs to the list!

1

"HOW TO CHANGE STUFF WITHOUT BLOWING IT UP"

SIGN: THE FIRECRACKER

By Andy McQuitty

If it's true that the only people who like change are wet babies, it follows that Pastors who make changes will generally be vilified by the greater bulk of their congregation who don't wear diapers or wet their pants.

This concept is a significant problem since change is one of life's fundamental constants. The second constant—the nearly universal resistance of human beings to the first constant—makes change threatening and unpleasant to most people.

When trains were first invented, experts opposed their use. They feared that, at the frightful speed of 15 m.p.h., passengers would get nosebleeds and suffocate when going through tunnels. Some church people have similar fears about launching a new building program.

But change has always come to churches, and I think it's safe to say it always will. In fact, it must. If our churches and ministries have any hope for continued growth and health in decades to come, it is founded on a willingness to take the "status" out of the "quo". In a rapidly changing world, any institution that is through changing…is through.

My Hobo sign here is the Firecracker: beware blowing stuff up when you can just change it. But I hasten to add this corollary: also beware of too-hasty change, and no change at all. The important thing to pursue is appropriate change, and that begins by embracing God's perspective on change. Genesis 1.1 describes the most incredible change in history. "In the beginning, God created the Heavens and the earth." I maintain that going from no universe to our universe in the space of seven days was a rather dramatic alteration in eternity's status quo. We learn a simple from this change: God Almighty is an infinitely creative being. It is in His nature to innovate, to multiply, and to diversify. That's why no two snowflakes are identical, and no two people are alike. That's why birds and animals and plant life come in all shapes, sizes and colors. That's why no two church members will agree on how loud the music should be or what color the nursery should be painted.

Changing things may be scary. Changing things may be difficult. But changing things is part of how God rolls. "Behold, the former things have come to pass, now I declare new things; before they spring forth I proclaim them to you. Sing to the Lord a new song, sing His praise from the end of the earth " (Isaiah 42.9-10). Just consider some of God's "new "things:

"a new song in our mouths" (Ps. 40.3)

"a new covenant" (Jer.31.31)

"a new heart and spirit" (Ez. 18.31)

"a new commandment" (Jn. 13.34)

"a new creature" (2 Cor. 5.17)

"a new man" (Eph. 4.24)

"a new heaven and earth" (Rev. 21.1)

"Behold, I am making all things new" (Rev. 21.5)

Change is the natural corollary of God's creativity. From the beginning, He created a universe which was to be fluid, not static; innovative, fresh, and diverse, not stolid, rigid, and monolithic. In fact, change is the engine of growth. God's original commands to the first human beings involved a quest for growth through change: "multiply your descendants and subdue the earth." To grow in these ways by definition necessitated change.

But that doesn't mean the average pastor still won't get whacked by the powerful contingent (in every church) of steady-state conservatives who see spiritual merit in embracing flat-earth cosmology.

These folks have more interest in preserving programs than effectively propagating the gospel or meeting needs. They have a maintenance mindset, but not motivation to make things better. They are more concerned about form than function. They are more wrapped up in the church's past glories than focused on future impact, more motivated by conformity than creativity, by reputation than responsibility, by memories than dreams.

I have a pastor friend who said that it would be easier in his church to change the doctrinal statement than the order of worship. That congregation is confusing essentials and nonessentials: as they slowly replace gospel with tradition. When the United States was largely agrarian and farmers had cows to milk, they could only make it to service if scheduled at 11. And, since it was such a hassle to hitch the team and travel to church, they stayed all day and into the night. Now many Americans believe the God-appointed time for worship on Sunday is 11 A.M., and that all faithful churches have services on Sunday night! The sad thing is many don't even know how these "convictions" emanate not from scripture, but from the mammary glands of eighteenth-century cows.

The modern church tends to be saddled with a wide variety of such highly volatile traditional but non-biblical albatrosses. Think with me now. I'm going to throw out some concepts, and you decide whether they are absolute values or matters of subjective taste: the gospel message, the color of carpet in the sanctuary, the deity of Christ, whether the choir wears robes or not, excellence in all we do to the glory of God, using only piano and organ in worship, worshipping God with dignity and reverence, the times our services are held, serving and loving others in tangible ways, the publisher we use for Sunday School material, platform people in jeans or hatless in coats and ties...

One of Jesus' genius (read, "divine") leadership practices was clearly demarcating the essential from the optional. His methods and emphases were so creative and unique that His enemies accused Him of breaking God's law. But no. Jesus was fulfilling the Law, not breaking it. His methods were innovative, but His convictions of the truth were unchanging. He had perfect balance. Like Him, leaders today can't allow "nay-changer's" knee-jerk opposition to sabotage positive attitudes that welcome needed change. Therefore, they need to learn how to wisely introduce change in such a way that it doesn't blow everything to smithereens. Allow me to offer a few anti-explosive thoughts along these lines.

First, the limitation of change in Christian ministry is truth. Scripture-endorsed changes must be tempered by knowing what never changes. For example, God's character never changes. "Thou...in the beginning didst lay the foundation of the earth, and the heavens are the works of thy hands; they will perish, but Thou remainest; and they all will become old as a garment...they will also be changed... but Thou art the same, and Thy years will not come to an end" (Heb. 1.10-12, Nice touch there using the King James to make the some-things-never-change point, don't you think?). God's creativity is a quality which, while producing change in His universe, is itself part of His never-changing character. Things may change, but God never does.

Neither does God's truth. Remember Jesus' words in Mt. 5.17-18? "Do not think that I came to abolish the Law or the Prophets; I did not come to abolish, but to fulfill...for until heaven and earth pass away, not the smallest letter or stroke shall pass away from the Law, until all is accomplished." The principles of God's Word simply do not change from age to age or culture to culture; His truth is sure, absolute, and immutable.

For Christian leaders, this means that is it valid for us only to alter forms, not functions; programs, not principles; techniques, not truths. In our day, many mainline churches are violating these rules. In the interest of "relevance" and "progress", they are altering God's truth in a futile effort to garner popularity with the public square. And so, they've jettisoned the doctrine of Hell, the deity of Christ, the coming judgment, the sanctity of human life, and the gospel itself. In so doing, they've violated the primary limitation of change—truth itself.

Not cool. Actually, it is. Such appeasement doesn't explode churches. It freezes them. Very cool. Frozen actually!

Second, the rationale for change is effectiveness. Jesus hinted at this when He said in Luke 5.37-28: "And no one puts new wine into old wineskins; otherwise the new wine will burst the skins, and it will be spilled out, and the skins will be ruined. But new wine must be put into fresh wineskins." Jesus is teaching that the wine of the gospel is new and fresh in each generation. To keep the unchanging gospel message effective in every age, we must package it in new and fresh ways. We can't cling to the forms of expression of previous generations. We need new ways that communicate, ways that make a difference. Some Christians believe pragmatism is a vice, but Paul didn't. In 1 Cor. 9.20-22, he wrote: "...though I am free from all men, I have made myself a slave to all, that I might win the more...I have become all things to all men, that I may by all means save some. And I do all things for the sake of the gospel, that I may become a fellow partaker of it." Paul doesn't change his message; he simply tailors its packaging to make it as effective as possible to a particular audience. As for Paul, the sole focus for change ought always to be increased effectiveness in accomplishing our purpose of building God's kingdom.

Resisting change that would increase effectiveness just to maintain the status quo is irrational. If it *is* broke, fix it. Many churches today are addressing the issues of the 1920's with the methods of the 1950"s to people living in the 2020's. Their motto is, "Come weal, come woe, our status is quo." Their favorite benediction is the one that ends, "As it has been, so shall it ever be—world without end, AMEN." We need to wean ourselves of the mistaken assumption that there's only one right way of doing things.

Instead, we should discipline ourselves to think vicariously from the perspective of those we're trying to reach. What attracts? What communicates? What *works*? I was raised on some of the great old hymns. But in some settings, they just don't communicate to the modern mind. Take an average church audience today and sing, "There is a balm in Gilead", and somebody will be thinking, "I hope they get it diffused before it blows." Sing, "All hail the power of Jesus' name, let angels prostrate fall" and somebody will think: "That angel better get on a regimen of saw palmetto." The message just doesn't come across.

Now I love those old hymns. But the question is not what I love, but what communicates. We should remember that Martin Luther set the words of "A Mighty Fortress" to a contemporary barroom tune of his day. Today's traditional hymns are yesterday's contemporary songs.

With an understanding of this ever-shifting message, we need to embrace changes that will help us be more effective. Someone has aptly said that the seven last words of the church are: "But we've always done it that way." Perhaps that attitude is at the root of the sad stat that 85% of the churches in America are either static or declining in terms of membership. Folks, the great tragedy here is that the church has a life-giving message that can't get though because it refuses to change to more effective methods.

Finally, the attitude of change must be unselfishness. Paul wrote in Phil. 2.3,4: "Do nothing from selfishness or empty conceit, but with humility of mind let each of you regard one another as more important than himself; do not merely look out for your own personal interests, but also for the interests of others." Jesus' example teaches that God is pleased with those who unselfishly submit their preferences to changes that will benefit others.

Fact one: in a growing church, no one person will have everything their way (believe me—that definitely includes the pastor, too). Let me just ask you, in your family, do you have total agreement on every issue? When you go out to eat, do all the kids and adults want to go to the same restaurant? When you go on vacation, does everybody want to do the same thing? No way. Now if, in a family, not everyone can be totally pleased, what makes us think that's possible in a church? It isn't. There will be those who prefer traditional approaches and those who prefer contemporary approaches, and both groups will need to flex.

Fact two: God is pleased when a spirit of unselfishness prevails among His people. He will respond to people's unselfishness by doing great things in their midst. Just think of John the Baptist. What would have happened had he said: "Wait a second; I like things the way they are. I have all these disciples following me, all these big wigs from Jerusalem coming out to see me, and the attention of King Herod himself. I don't think I'll move aside for Jesus, after all." But he didn't. He saw that Christ was what the world needed; he was only the forerunner. And so, as John unselfishly yielded his place, Christ did increase, and God brought salvation to the world.

Let's commit ourselves to evaluate changes, not in terms of inconvenience to ourselves, but in terms of benefit to the Body as a whole. Let's be unselfish about our preferences, focusing on our purposes. If we do, God will do great things in our midst. So how do we go about leading such change?

First, create a sense of discontent with what must be changed. It is almost impossible to overstate the importance of discontent. Without discontent in the present situation there can be no intentional and internally motivated change. Unhappy that we are not growing?

Unhappy that we are losing our young people? Unhappy that we are becoming irrelevant? Own that! To overcome natural anti-change inertia, leaders have to stoke the fire of discontent in the hearts of their people.

Second, cast vision. To create purposeful movement, leaders must channel the often-frenetic human motion of change toward a specific end. When things seem to be falling apart, leaders paint a picture of the exciting new world we can create from the pieces. Out of uncertainty, leaders must describe a new future that pulls the organization together.

Last, invite people into the movement. Folks who are fired up by causes are energized. They put their hearts into their work. They "buy in" to change. Provide your people a grand purpose, a mission with a larger meaning, a cause that transcends the dullness of their everyday duties. Give them a dream they can identify with and watch commitment climb.

In over three decades of ministry in one church, I've seen much change. As far as I can tell, we made those changes without blowing everything up. Sure, there was some singeing and smoke and soot. We lost people with virtually every change. But we avoided the Big Bang, and the church went forward and prospered.

We've changed our dress code (suits and ties to jeans), our preaching schedule (all exposition to topical series to lectionary), our preaching approach (senior pastor to teaching team, from one to six), our altar time (from non-existent to every week with candles and prayer intercessors), our visuals (from words on screen to rich imagery), our mission focus (from sending to foreign fields to everyone a missionary out of the box), our music (from choirs and organs and robes to worship bands), our view of women's roles in ministry (from teaching kids and women-only to preaching and leading), our ministry emphasis (from knowing lots of stuff to doing lots of stuff with what we know), our staff organization (from hierarchical to teams), our elder board role (from micromanaging to overseeing from altitude), our physical address (from a declining sector of our city to a thriving one), our facilities (from traditional to highly creative and community-welcoming), our hiring practices (from standard reference searches to full on group interviews), and our sermon planning (from one harried pastor to a creative team).

There is no growth without challenge, and no challenge without change. The bad news is that change is hard, and people don't like it. The good news is that appropriate change is good, and it can be accomplished. So, watch your back and pick up the drawing board and you'll discover that, when it's all been said and done, babies aren't really the only ones who embrace a good change!

RESPONSE TO:
THE FIRECRACKER

By Larry Parsley

As I read the closing paragraphs of your essay, Andy, I could almost hear the theme from *Rocky* in the background. You reminded me that one of the most important and under-appreciated roles of the pastor is to be a "change agent." There were so many points that resonated with me.

First, I agreed with the crucial necessity of changing the *right* things. I am sadly familiar with churches whose robed choirs sing the same songs the same way they did 50 years ago, but who at the same time over these last 50 years have thrown huge, core doctrines overboard, because they didn't match up well with modernity.

Second, as you spoke, I was reminded of the old car commercial, where the wizened mechanic looks at the customer and says, "You can pay me now, or you can pay me later." That is certainly the reality that faces pastors. If we postpone the price of change now (thinking we will save ourselves pain) the really expensive bill comes later — when we wake up and find ourselves leading a church that does not look like its community and can't reach it. Such churches are museums and not vibrant mission outposts.

Third, I could not help but think of the mixed messages I've heard from pastoral search committees over the years ("We need someone who's going to come in and revitalize our worship and help us reach young people again"...AND..."Our church is pretty beat up by all the foolish innovations our previous pastor tried. We need a patient leader who will give us time to heal from past trauma"). The tough thing is that there is often truth in both messages; we need wisdom and courage to steer between them.

Fourth, I reflected on the wise counsel that I've received that *change has a price tag*, and that seasoned leaders need to think about a change budget. There are a few changes that will be relatively inexpensive *and* universally welcome. For example, it will not cost you too much to fire the gruff and ineffective receptionist who was hired in the transition between you and your predecessor. Most change, however, will cost a lot more leadership capital. If you can, think of change as an investment. Let the dividends of new changes fund the next strategic initiative. Don't get upside down on borrowing from your leadership capital if you can help it.

Lastly, Andy, I think the thing that spoke to me most about your essay was your list of significant changes that you've made in your tenure at Irving Bible Church. I'm going to guess that every one of those changes cost you something – long elder meetings, painful goodbye letters, email (!), hard phone conversations, and sleepless nights. But each one of those changes has helped to position your church to minister in the 21st century. Keep up the hard work!

2
PREACHING: THE MAGNIFICENT NIGHTMARE

By: Larry Parsley

The preaching event is a magnificent nightmare. The venerable preacher Gardner C. Taylor aptly spoke of the preaching life as "the sweet torture of Sunday morning." Which one of us deserves to speak on God's behalf? It is an incredible privilege to have several dozen or several hundred people (folks whom you highly respect) block out a good half hour to listen to you speak (*you*, of all people). Their time is valuable; their Sundays are precious. Yet there they sit, most of them *listening* to you, and some listening attentively. If you are wired like I am (that is, if you love the spiritual and creative alchemy of putting together a sermon), then the whole exercise of preaching is breathtaking.

But let's be honest. Preaching is a nightmare. The pace is relentless. If you preach a good 40+ Sunday sermons a year, you are never really *not* thinking about preaching.

First and foremost, preaching is a nightmare because it's laced with temptations to pride:

- How am I performing relative to my peer preachers in this community?
- Are my illustrations passionate but not overly emotional?
- Are my words gripping and relevant — but not cheesy?
- Am I funny, yet not silly?
- Am I drawing attention to myself?
- Is my interpretation of scripture exegetically and theologically sound?
- Am I standing within the orthodox interpretation of this text, yet still bringing a fresh word? Maybe even a word that no other preacher from this pulpit has ever divined from this text?
- Is my pacing right — not too rushed yet not too labored?
- Do I have too much eye contact, but not enough precision in my words (*ums* and *ahhs* and looping repetition)?
- Is my sermon too 'manuscripty' and 'essayish', and therefore not lively?
- Will my tears be mistaken for manipulation? Will my dry eyes be mistaken for spiritual dryness?
- If I don't share personal stories, illustrations and application, will the sermon seem academic and remote? If I do, will people think I'm showboating my piety?

With all of these considerations, preaching, in my experience, is a magnificent nightmare! What follows is a 'typical' week as a working preacher, complete with the joys and pains of the preaching life.

MONDAY

On Monday, I take a courier's packet and empty the contents onto my desk. I have tried to preach without the courier, the one who delivers to me on Mondays the title, text, and thesis for the sermon to come on Sunday. And I would spend Mondays, Tuesdays, Wednesdays, and sometimes Thursdays, searching for that elusive text, title, and thesis (with little time left over to actually prepare the sermon). That was miserable.

Several years into full-time preaching, my church blessed me with the gift of an annual study break (usually three weeks in July). That study break has served multiple purposes:

- Gives me a chance to detox from the pace of the previous ministry year
- Allows my kids to see Dad on a weekend with no sermon stress
- Affords me an opportunity to do some general reading and think about big-picture goals for the coming year.

But by far, the greatest value of the study break is to prepare the 'book' that will guide my preaching for the next year. This 'book' will take me through the holy seasons of Advent, Lent, and Easter, as well as more 'ordinary time' spent preaching biblical and topical sermon series. This preaching plan strives to balance Old Testament with New Testament, theological with practical, pastoral with prophetic, and challenge with promise. Suppose I do my work well and am blessed with God's anointing during those three weeks of summer study. In that case, the result is that every Monday morning, a courier knocks on my door and hands me the digital equivalent of a brown manila envelope — the contents of which are a *series title* and theme, a *sermon title*, at least one text of Scripture, and (if I'm lucky) a paragraph of explanation about how to preach this sermon.

On Mondays, I take the contents, drop them out on my desk and begin to sift through them. Applying an immutable law of homiletical wisdom, I never look at a commentary on Monday. I peer only at the scripture text itself. I play reverential games with it—cutting and pasting the digital text into Word documents and breaking the passage into sections, clauses, and phrases and words. I like to see the layout of the component pieces on the page. I'll make a logical outline of the text to try to see the flow of the argument.

Mondays are purely magnificent—just the Scripture text and me, and a whopping 6 days before I have to say something *inspired* about it.

TUESDAY

On Tuesdays, I take a field trip. I travel to seminaries and famous pulpits, usually of the late 20th-century variety. I poll what experts have had to say about my particular sermon text. On Tuesdays, a mind whetted with Monday's questions tries to find out:

- Now who again was Salome, and why was she at the empty tomb?
- What was significant about that road from Jerusalem to Jericho?
- Sometimes, I even search in vain for answers to deep questions: Why did God prefer Abel's sacrifice to Cain's?

On Tuesdays, I'm a sucker for etymology—I find it fascinating that the word Paul uses to describe Epaphras' 'wrestling' in prayer in Col 4:12 is 'agonizo' (i.e., 'agonizing' in prayer).

Tuesday has some scary bits as well. Eminent scholars and commentators disagree over key points of exegesis. With whom do I side? The one who suits my preconceived thesis the best? And what about the points commentators fail to weigh in on? Like, 'Why were the women in the tomb more afraid after the angel in the tomb told them Jesus was alive?' That seems to be a pretty key point to me—I'd like to build a whole sermon around that question, but none of the experts I consult have discussed this issue thoroughly, or at least not in a convincing fashion.

The nightmare of Tuesday is wondering if these deep mysteries can be solved or if my sermon will be more like the homiletical 'cold case.'

WEDNESDAY

I have one main task on Wednesdays, and it is mammoth: to produce a very rough draft of Sunday's sermon. I block out almost my entire workday to give to this task.

I take the notes I've made for myself on Monday and Tuesday, often printed out, sometimes scribbled out, and after a decent time, prayer, and a cup of coffee, I often head to a park near my house. Armed with my sheaf of notes and a digital recorder, I go for a four-mile walk, and dictate a rough draft of my sermon into that little machine. I fear I resemble someone either pompous or troubled as I talk to myself while walking around the park, but that doesn't matter. When I can get away from the commotion of the office and simply walk and talk out my sermon, it helps me overcome writer's block. I speak it out in short bursts of phrases and sentences, with lots of pauses on the recorder. It helps me to just get something out. Often, after four miles, I'm not done, and I must finish the rest of the audio draft in my car.

Still, it's great relief when I have an audio draft of my sermon.

Later, when transcribing it, I notice run-on sentences, poorly thought-out ideas, and annoying non-sequiturs. What hours earlier felt so stirring to me as I stared at geese on a pond, now feels imbalanced and convoluted.

I press on. I do my best to get those three-thousand words on paper, and often I am seeking to find the shape or outline in what I have dictated. I get it in some kind of shape and race to my office by 4:00 pm to meet with several members of our church staff. Then, after offering a lame apology, I read my draft to them in an awkward and rapid fashion. They are unfailingly gracious and gentle and almost always say something encouraging. Then they never fail to give me great feedback on what can be fixed.

It's a magnificent feeling to know, on Wed afternoon, that I could preach this sermon in its present form some four days from now. It wouldn't be good, but I could still preach something.

THURSDAY

On Thursdays, I feel struggle over all the things that I've neglected to do on Wednesday. Those twenty-four hours generate a lot of emails and issues to address. If I stay on schedule, on Thursday, I will take the sermon manuscript that I presented on Wed afternoon to my colleagues. This stapled draft is now festooned with questions, ideas, movie dialogue, and arrows. I do my best to fix the fatal flaws in the sermon.

FRIDAY

Friday is my day off. When all goes well, I finish up my revisions on Thursday, and Fridays are days of long walks or chores or lunches with my wife or sneaking in a few innings of watching baseball. But things don't always go well, and Fridays are sometimes 'catch-up' days.

SATURDAY

If there is a day to focus on delivery, it is Saturday. I may polish my manuscript. I like to make the rough places plain and embed hooks so that the sermon is easier for the congregation (and me!) to remember. On an uncomplicated Saturday, I will go for a walk with my sermon in hand and say it aloud to the wind and the trees.

Saturdays are often nightmare days. At times I am bored with my sermon. Or there is this one part that really bugs me, and I can't figure out how to fix it. Or I am nagged by the lack of a passionate conclusion. I wonder if I'll have to conclude the sermon with something on the order of, "Well, I could probably say a little more, but in the interest of time, how about we just stop right there and then we can begin anew next week." Not exactly a soaring conclusion!

SUNDAY

On Sundays, I set my alarm earlier than normal. I eat a decent breakfast and drink a strong cup of coffee. I try not to let my anxiety about fiddling with my sermon tempt me to preempt my morning devotion time. When I'm on my game, I have a rich and leisurely time of prayer and Bible reading. I snack on psalms, epistles and OT stories of faith, as well as red-letter admonitions and promises. When my prayer time is going well, I seize upon a verse or phrase from my devotional reading that morning that becomes my trapeze rope, a Biblical promise I cling to during the challenges of the morning.

Then I drive to church. I turn once again to that sermon. It's surprising how, either through the inspiration of the Spirit or the cold sweats of a fast-approaching deadline, new insights will reveal themselves to me. I'm consistently amazed how notes that are jotted down in the margin mere minutes before the sermon begins become the most talked about points.

After another verbal rehearsal, I meet with a half-dozen to a dozen 'prayer partners.' I present in a few minutes the main contours of the sermon. I point out areas where I need specific prayer. My friends intercede, and it is never *not* an uplifting experience. Five minutes before the first worship service begins, I fire up a 'Geronimo!' prayer (the kind of prayer a paratrooper prays when exiting the plane) and enter the sanctuary.

The half-hour of worship that precedes my sermon feels anything but tranquil. Anxiety over my sermon and self-consciousness of people watching me (everybody watches the preacher during the worship service) are confronted by honest attempts to sing the songs and extol my Savior.

I'm truly relieved when I finally ascend the stage and stand behind the pulpit. I rise to give voice to this Word that has been germinating in me all week. I prayerfully apply the scalpel of sharp truth. I stand to discharge my primary duty as a pastor. Now is the time to unleash the Word of God.

Preaching is magnificent. Preaching is a nightmare. Preaching is a magnificent nightmare.

As soon as the service is done, I stand in the middle of our church lobby, far enough from the exit where people don't feel compelled to shake my hand and tell me they liked the sermon (whether they did or not), but close enough to dialogue with people about spiritual matters or routine chit chat.

It is always magnificent to hear how God used this message on this particular day to speak a timely word to someone starved for it. But as I drive home, I am hit with regrets. Why did I zig instead of zag, homiletically speaking? Why did my voice choke up when sharing that personal story? Why didn't my voice have more passion? Did I speak as 'a dying man to dying men,' as one Puritan put it so well, or did I give an interesting little religious talk? Sunday afternoons can be a real nightmare.

"But no matter," I tell myself as Sundays draw to a close, "there's always next week."

RESPONSE TO:
THE ALARMCLOCK

By: Andy McQuitty

Larry bravely wrote "On Saturday nights, I'm ashamed to admit, I have been known to 'google' phrases like "John Ortberg tells the story". But not, "Andy McQuitty tells the story"? Don't worry partner, I'll get over it! (I wouldn't google me, either)

Just reading Larry's recitation of a week's worth of sermon preparation was enough to make my PTSD (Post Traumatic Sermon Disorder) erupt, and here it's Friday when things should be settling down. So, you know he struck a chord! There's no doubt about it: preaching is a pastor's single most magnificent recurring nightmare assignment. That's not because the preacher dislikes preaching. On the contrary, it's because he absolutely loves it but often feels the pressure of the for-the-preacher-every-other-day-is-Sunday syndrome: "I dread what I love because I feel like I have to do it so often that I can't do it well".

I daresay few people who hear our sermons have the slightest concept of the blood, sweat, and tears that were spent to craft them. It's not just old-fashioned elbow grease that goes into it. Preachers scoff at the mere threat of hard work. It's the churning doubts and desperate fears and roiling uncertainty and relentless self-doubt and never-ending quest added to that hard work that puts us under the table. It's not that we don't want to be fatigued. It's that we don't want to be embarrassed.

When I first began full-time preaching in 1987, I thought it would be rather like writing a college term-paper and presenting it on Sunday. That expectation was only partly true. Preaching does begin with writing a term-paper once a week, but it's way more than just presenting that paper. Preaching is more like writing a term paper once a week while having your teeth drilled at the dentist, and then presenting your work to an American Idol crowd with a final verdict given publicly by an indigestion-afflicted Simon Cowell.

Hence, PTSD.

But I hasten to add hope to the nightmare. Over the years, I've noticed that preachers with staying power (like my friend Larry) have developed three assets that they utilize weekly in staying happy, healthy, and productive even in the magnificent nightmare. Here they are, in order.

1. ***Realistic expectations:*** you are neither perfect nor sinless. You weren't last week. You won't be next week. And you KNOW you're not this week. So be realistic in your expectations *for* and your evaluations *of* yourself. Before I preached regularly, I thought that 100% heart purity was the *sina qua non* of God-blessed oratory. I quickly learned to settle for 50% (or less) when I realized that if I waited to preach before my motives and my thoughts were totally pure, I'd simply NEVER preach. But I'm called to preach, so I suspect the good Lord factored this imperfection problem into my performance. Don't look at me that way. I know 50% is low, but hey, it's honest and, more importantly, realistic. So next week, become a godlier preacher. But right now, get up there and preach! (And endeavor always to get to 60% at least ASAP)

2. ***Repeatable disciplines:*** Larry's method for sermon prep is nothing short of magnificent. All of his steps are probably not right for everyone who preaches, though. We all need to find our own rhythms and disciplines (I don't think I could make an audio manuscript from scratch no matter how many lakes I walked around. And if I did manage it, I would probably have a conniption when I listened to it back in the saner environs of my hopefully private study.) But Larry's disciplined process is genius because he's built it to order over the years and it is repeatable and it works for him just like practicing scales does for a concert pianist.

3. ***Relaxed relinquishment:*** Every preacher always wishes they could have another shot at some portion of or sentence in their sermons. But unfortunately, we all know there's no such thing as a preaching mulligan and that the best decision to take regarding that fanciful idea is to relinquish it. For myself, I've found the best way to do that is to repeat the prayer my wife and I have lettered on a plaque hanging in our kitchen: *"Pray hard, work hard, trust God."* Amen. If you prayed that sermon through and prepared it with hard work and preached it with passion, then you've succeeded and now you're free to relinquish all regrets about inevitable imperfections in your message. It's in God's hands now and you can trust Him to make sure that what He just said through you doesn't come back void.

After all of that, ponder one of Larry's most encouraging sentences in this whole chapter: "No matter, there's always next week."

3

DON'T SWEAT THE SMALL STUFF

By: Andy McQuitty

Being of Irish extraction (and therefore fond of recommending to my friends Thomas Cahill's profoundly true book, *How the Irish Saved Civilization*), I often receive Irish jokes from said friends, inexplicably of a somewhat derogatory nature. Here's one that came recently that seems to contain a moral dilemma for a dear Irish Catholic sister:

"Sitting by the window of her convent, Sister Barbara opened a letter from home one evening. Inside the letter was a $100 bill her parents had sent. Sister Barbara smiled at the gesture. As she read the letter by the window, she noticed a shabbily dressed stranger leaning against the lamp post below. Quickly, she wrote, "Don't despair. Sister Barbara," on a piece of paper, wrapped the $100 bill in it, got the man's attention and tossed it out the window to him. The stranger picked it up, and with a puzzled ex-

pression and a tip of his hat, went off down the street. The next day, Sister Barbara was told that a man was at her door, insisting on seeing her. She went down and found the stranger waiting. Without a word, he handed her a huge wad of $100 bills. "What's this?" she asked. "That's the $8,000 you have coming Sister," he replied. "Don't Despair paid 80-to-1."

Some would say that sister Barbara has unwittingly committed a venal sin by winning at the ponies and needs to proceed straight to confession after returning the money. Why? Because Sister Barbara is a Christian, and everybody knows good Christians never wager on horses. Or if they do, they surely aren't allowed to win.

Really? How does everyone know that? Well, because everybody just does. My fellow Hobos, there are certain activities that Christians don't do, not necessarily because God explicitly condemns them, but because current Christian culture and tradition do. "I don't drink, smoke, and chew. . . or go with girls who do." Fine. But has God truly forbidden you to do so (assuming you have a girlfriend who spits in a cup)? It may not be smart or attractive or prudent to do such things, but is the decision not to engage really a measure of spiritual maturity?

Here's my beef. I hate it that we've allowed Christianity to be defined by outward things we're forbidden to do instead of by profound, God-ordained things we're supposed to do. Jesus had choice words for some Pharisees who so warped the essence of true spirituality:

"You're hopeless, you religion scholars and Pharisees! Frauds! You keep meticulous account books, tithing on every nickel and dime you get, but on the meat of God's Law, things like fairness and compassion and commitment—the absolute basics! —you carelessly take it or leave it. Careful bookkeeping is commendable, but the basics are required..."You're hopeless, you religion scholars and Pharisees! Frauds!

You burnish the surface of your cups and bowls so they sparkle in the sun, while the insides are maggoty with your greed and gluttony. Stupid Pharisee! Scour the insides, and then the gleaming surface will mean something (Matt 23:23-26).

Those guys were meticulous on the superficial stuff but bailed on what really mattered. Why? Because it was easier for them to keep book on tithes than it was to show compassion. It's easier for us, too. It's easier to swear off a stogie than it is to treat someone fairly when it costs us something. It's easier not to put a quarter in a slot machine than to be committed heart and soul to the cause of Jesus Christ. So, what happens? We subtly tend to define Christianity by external stuff we don't do because that's easier than bellying up to the challenge of doing what God really wants: love Him with our heart, soul, mind, strength, and our neighbor as ourselves! How weird is it that the perverted values of the Pharisees in Jesus' day keep cropping up in modern Christianity? In some church circles, you can be a self-righteous, arrogant, gossipy, back-stabbing jerk and qualify as a church leader, but the minute you drink a cold beer with pizza you're a persona non grata. What's up with that? Does *not doing* stuff really equate to God-honoring spirituality? If so, then a corpse wins the morality contest hands down because it never does *anything*!

How many folks who would truly love to know Jesus are turned off by dour legalists who forbid what God has never forbidden and thereby sully the true nature of our faith? How many spiritual seekers never get past the teetotalistic (made up word!) severity of modern-day Pharisees who present Christianity as a religion whose goal is to suck every bit of joy from life through hair-splitting rules?

Can you tell? I'm on a crusade against this shallow, intelligence-insulting brand of Christian legalism. It's just too tempting to resort to pseudo-spiritual fluff like this than to do the hard work of serv-anthood. I say we revolt against the Pharisaical spirit and hit a lick for true spirituality. In my mind, our task is two-fold. 1) Get serious about serious stuff. 2) Don't sweat the small stuff.

More on that first rule, people who don't follow Jesus know the real deal when they see it! If Christians live selfless, giving, generous, humble, compassionate, joyful, positive, patient, courageous lives, that's going to appeal to the soul and conscience of all who see them. This appeal is especially powerful if the Christian is living this way without the artificial pomposity of arbitrary rules-keeping.

When it comes to the second rule, this is where I'm going to catch the most flack! Don't sweat the small stuff. If you're like me and think it's fine if, in moderation, you want to enjoy a cold beer with pizza, or light up a stogie every so often (especially if you can score a Cuban), or sip a fine pinot noir with your dinner—then you should do so gratefully, guiltlessly, and joyfully! Please hear me! I'm not recommending social drinking, or cigar-smoking, or wine-sipping, or entertainment-wagering. I own no stock in Cohiba, and I think using the lottery to fund public education is a bad idea and I think it's dumb (if not sinful, c.f. 1 Corinthians 6:18-20) to ruin your health with cigarette addiction. And for those who may be predisposed by family history, genetics, or personal disposition to addictive behavior with regard to alcohol, tobacco or gambling, by all means exercise wisdom and stay far, far away from these potentially destructive temptations in your life.

But can the rest of us just not get our underwear in a wad about this stuff? When we do, it only makes people around us think Christians are weird and hope they're never taken with an irresistible urge to become one! I'd much rather see us as believers speaking the truth in love and keeping our hearts pure and becoming selfless servants of God and others and celebrating at the end of the day with a prayer/praise meeting at church and later enjoying a fine Merlot at my house

OK. I hear you asking (or yelling?) some questions. Slow down and let me respond one at a time. Thanks!

First, "What does God think about this?" Well, He's pretty clear on overindulgence of any kind, whether it's eating or drinking or anything. For example, the abuse of alcohol is specifically condemned. It is clear, "be not drunk with wine" (Eph 5.18), and that entails moderation and temperance (1 Tim. 3.2).

But assuming there is control and moderation, God delights in His children's enjoyment of fine things. He hates the legalistic spirit that reduces spirituality to forbidding good gifts given by God. This is the essence of Phariseeism, a moral standard insidious not only because it erects arbitrary external standards for righteousness, but because in so doing it distracts from what is truly precious to God's heart. Yes, God hates the abuse of alcohol. But I believe He hates even more the denial of the proper use of alcohol as a false standard of spirituality that results in straining at gnats and swallowing camels (Matt. 23.23-24). Thus, consider 1 Tim. 4:1-5:

". . . deceiving spirits . . . whose consciences have been seared as with a hot iron. . . forbid people to marry and order them to abstain from certain foods, which God created to be received with thanksgiving by those who believe and who know the truth. For everything God created is good, and nothing is to be rejected if it is received with thanksgiving, because it is consecrated by the word of God and prayer."

One of Satan's most effective strategies is to make Christians look backward, foolish, and joyless in the eyes of unbelieving people by embracing legalistic standards that have nothing to do with true spirituality. God wants us to enjoy life fully, and that includes thankfully enjoying His good gifts in those times when we are privileged to receive them. As the above scripture notes, history is full of false teachers who wrongly condemn as unspiritual the enjoyment of things like a fine Chateau Briand, a mellow merlot, chocolate mousse, veal piccatta, or an ice-cold beer with fajitas after a hot afternoon on the golf course. I am not one of them, and I think God is happy about that. I know I am. Next question please.

"What does this do for the cause of Christ? . . . particularly since you are God's representative?"

This is the inevitable "preacher" question which wrongly assumes that pastors have a greater responsibility to honor God with their lives than other believers. I'll answer the question, but only after observing that we're all on the hook together when it comes to walking uprightly!

As God's representative, I am dutybound to represent God accurately. If God is pleased when we properly enjoy His good gifts, then I believe I represent Him well by properly enjoying His good gifts. The question implies that if people knew that I enjoyed a cold beer or a fine glass of wine or a nice stogie on occasion, they would be turned off to the cause of Christ. But I disagree. My responsibility as a pastor is to live authentically and biblically, not artificially or Pharisaically. I have found that doing so, far from putting people off to Jesus, actually frees people around me to focus on issues that really matter to Jesus' heart. That is precisely what Paul concludes in 1 Tim. 4:6:

"If you point these things out to the brothers [that " everything God created is good, and nothing is to be rejected if it is received with thanksgiving"], you will be a good minister of Christ Jesus, brought up in the truths of the faith and of the good teaching that you have followed."

Any other questions?

"What will you tell your children when they are tempted to indulge? Will your actions encourage wrong behavior? Will you be a stumbling block?"

Not to be redundant, but it's wrong to abuse alcohol or cigars or fine food or anything else, and that is what I teach my kids. As to being a stumbling block, that occurs through two scenarios: if I abuse these things, or if I encourage someone else to abuse them. Lord willing, I will never do either.

The practical question here, it seems to me, is how best to lead others with respect to potentially dangerous activities. Some believe we best serve our children and our friends by pushing total abstention. Thus, alcohol can be abused, therefore we forbid all use of alcohol. But cars can be driven too fast, causing accidents and even deaths; do we therefore forbid all use of cars? Desserts can be overeaten, causing obesity and heart disease; do we therefore forbid all desserts? Pain killers after surgery can become addictive if overused; do we therefore forbid all painkillers after surgery? Of course not.

Obviously, the wise goal is not to protect and lead in these issues by teaching denial, but by teaching responsibility. Total denial may seem safer for our kids, but I believe it is potentially destructive in the long run because of the "forbidden fruit" syndrome. Curiosity killed the cat, and it inevitably jumps up at young people at some point in their lives when, having entered adulthood, what has always been condemned and denied to them is suddenly available. Unfortunately, those who have merely been denied and not taught sometimes go off the deep end under those circumstances. It is my fervent hope that my children will not only avoid the "forbidden fruit" syndrome by my open but responsible enjoyment of potentially abused activities, but that they will learn how to live wisely and well as they observe moderation.

By the way, I think Sister Barbara should tithe her winnings gratefully and then take all the sisters to Disneyworld ASAP where I'll meet them personally for a fine wine tasting and a nice Partegas (robusto, please)!

Love God. Love people. Love life. Carpe diem. Bye bye. . .

RESPONSE TO:
THE MOLEHILL

By: Larry Parsley

I knew I was going to love this chapter when my favorite Irish friend opened with an excerpt from one of my favorite Irish writers involving a story about a gambling Irish nun! But that was only the beginning. I really fell in love with the chapter when Andy focused his laser pointer on one of the greatest obstacles the church faces – Herself!

In some ways, it is comforting to know that the modern-day church did not invent "sweating the small stuff." That sinful pattern is at least 2000 years old, as Andy pointed out from Matthew 23. But in other ways, it is so discouraging to see that churches have had two millennia to learn this lesson, yet we continue to major on minors and minor on majors. As a lifelong Baptist, I especially felt the sting of these prophetic words burning in all the right places.

And yet, I do want to offer a word of warning to my fellow Hobo's: what Andy advocates here will not be easy for most of us (depending upon the traditions of the churches where find ourselves). Why?

First, it is a lot easier to major on the minors. They are clear, easily measured, and easily enforced. The majors, on the other hand, such as "*justice, mercy and faithfulness,*" are all-encompassing pursuits, and not nearly as easily quantified or achieved.

Second, "sweating the small stuff" will be thought by many in your congregation to be your primary responsibility. In other words, your critics may try to hit you at one of your supposed strengths. "He calls himself a pastor, and yet he watches those movies, hangs out with those people, engages in those unrighteous appetites. What kind of preacher have we hired?"

But "don't despair" (as Sister Barbara might put it). Follow the godly counsel that Andy proposes and you will move toward reducing one of the greatest obstacles in reaching un-churched people. It is the goodness of creation that causes seekers to look heavenward and search for a Creator. And it is the qualitative dimension of *"justice, mercy and faithfulness"* that people find within your congregation that invites them to make a connection between the Christ who walks the pages of the Gospels and the living Christ who somehow manages to reveal Himself through His imperfect followers.

4

THE FUNERAL COMMITTEE

SIGN: THE CASKET

By: Larry Parsley

The news can come to you in so many different ways – a knock on your office door, a mid-meeting text, a call while you are at little league practice, or your home phone ringing way past midnight. But when that call comes and informs you that someone in your church has died, chances are that everything in your life will change over the next 72 hours. And depending upon the person and situation, there is a very good chance that every member of the "Funeral Committee" will be called into action. And by "Funeral Committee," I mean you.

One of the great surprises of my ministry is the spiritual potency of a funeral. But most likely, God's power will not flow through those who view this time as a clerical task to be quickly dispatched.

That's where the "Funeral Committee" comes in. As you try to do your day job, you are going to need to morph into a variety of different people to accomplish what the family and your church and your community need from at this moment. It will demand everything you have!

So what do I mean by that? Well let's take a look at some of the roles you will have to fill.

COMMUNITY ORGANIZER

First, you are going to need to become a community organizer. If the death was especially tragic, or sudden, or involved someone young, or a key stakeholder in your church, chances are your congregation and community will experience a kind of corporate shock. Grief will rob them of clear thinking.

And in many cases, you or someone you delegate will have to do their initial thinking for them. Funeral homes will need to be contacted. Calendars will need to be checked. Sound people and soloists and parking committees and former pastors will need to be consulted. A date and time for the visitation and the burial and the memorial service(s) will need to be set. And no one will be in the mental frame of mind to make sharp decisions. But you must be.

In some cases, almost everyone will want to contribute something—like enough casseroles to feed a developing nation for a month! Everyone wants to help, but not all help is helpful. You have to get the ball rolling as you and your staff and leaders help give organization and structure to the grieving process for the family and the congregation.

GOD'S RECEPTIONIST

Next, there's a good chance you may need to serve a role I like to call "God's receptionist." When death comes suddenly and tragically, inevitably many people will have lots of urgent questions for the manager – in this case, God. But they may often find God to be somewhat inaccessible to their requests for information. Since they don't feel like they can contact God directly, they will call you. After all, aren't you always at the switchboard?

You may find yourself taking a lot of calls, asking people if you can put them on hold (for 20 years or so) or telling them, "I am certain that God will get back to you at his earliest convenience." After 50 calls you will want to quit. Don't.

CONFESSOR

And then, don't be surprised if you find yourself in the position of "Father Confessor." Deaths prompt guilt.

I should've been a better parent.

I should've been a better spouse.

I should have been a better Deacon.

I should have been a better friend.

I should have been a better son or daughter.

I should have reached out.

I shouldn't have been so hard line.

I should have been firmer.

I should have gotten a second opinion.

I should have seen this coming.

I should have done something, said something, prayed something.

"Bless me father, for I have sinned." And some have. And some haven't. And you will need to listen to confessions, regardless of what church tradition you find yourself in.

JOURNALIST

And then, as you prepare to speak at the funeral, you will be called upon to play the role of journalist. Please don't be that pastor who merely reads the clergy record, a family email or two, and then trots out a tried-and-true funeral message. Show the deceased some respect!

Let their life speak—even the tragic parts, if you can. Try to assemble the closest family members in a room, and ask big questions.

What made him tick?

What were the great loves of his life?

What were the turning points in his life?

When did faith first begin to stir (if it ever stirred at all)?

What qualities (that are worth mentioning) has he passed on to his children?

These questions help me find the real man hiding behind the obituary; they open up opportunities to trigger holy memories and find grace flowing in the 'clay pot' of the deceased.

THEOLOGIAN

And of course, the theologian will need to be called in. It may be that the person you bury shared the same faith that characterizes the best of your congregation. If that is the case, glory be to God. But chances are, in many situations, you will face an absence of orthodox theology.

Indeed, increasingly, I find a sort of generic, optimistic deism at work among the bereaved. I meet family members who have no qualms about getting up on stage during a funeral and proclaiming that their loved one is now happy and thriving in a custom-built heaven.

I bet daddy is on the front nine right now, playing golf with St. Peter.

Bubba finally owns that NASCAR dream car and is racing around heaven's track.

I'm sure mom is in heaven right now, nudging the Angels out of the kitchen, fixing up some of her famous peach cobbler.

Now, layer a little of that over an essentially orthodox faith, and it is fairly harmless. But substitute if for Biblical faith, and it is deadly. As uncomfortable as it might be, you will be called upon to not only eulogize the deceased, but also to open the Book and expound upon its contents.

MASTER OF CEREMONIES

And then there is the underappreciated job of "Emcee." In most cases, the service must be put together. You will likely be called upon to do some gentle negotiation with family members over the architecture of the funeral service.

Will there be music?

What kind of music?

Who plays and who sings?

Who speaks?

And perhaps more importantly, how much time should they be allotted?

And even more importantly, how can we help them not overspend their time budget?

Is there a slide show?

Will there be a release of balloons or doves?

Will people wear colored ribbons?

You will be charged with the challenging task of putting together service that honors God, pays tribute to the loved one, gives the bereaved comfort and hope, and gets people out of there in less than three hours!

OPEN-AIR PREACHER

I remember reading with fascination about the famed preacher George Whitefield, and the success he achieved in a particular type of gospel proclamation. He would climb to a high vantage point, and preach for hours to the thousands who gathered. Whitfield's theological and theatrical prowess, combined with a heart for God and for the lost, rendered him a powerful force.

Times have certainly changed since the 1700s. Climb on top of a dumpster and start to preach, and there is a good chance that someone will call the cops.

Many pastors lack Whitfield's access to a cross-section of society: unchurched as well as churched. I have come to believe that funerals are the new "open-air preaching" that might have once been atop a wagon. Put a casket in a room and surround it with flowers and mourners, climb up on stage, and you will be granted the opportunity to speak to people from all segments of your community.

Now, I don't mean to be misunderstood. I'm not talking about hijacking a funeral and turning it into some kind of evangelistic rally. The mourners have come for a eulogy, and they deserve one. This occasion, however, is an opportunity, not simply for good words to be spoken about the deceased, but for gospel words to be spoken to all. For many who attend a funeral, it will feel like Death is God. Death always wins. Death swallows up everything we love.

And God has placed you there, in the "open air," if you will. And for this moment, you are Elijah on Mount Carmel. You are Paul, in the Areopagus. You are the prophet and the poet. You are the chronicler and the sage. And you have come to pay witness to the One who swallows up death and doles out hope.

I think you will see it takes a whole 'committee' to pull off a good funeral. And chances are, you will have to do all these things while simultaneously mourning the loss of this member of your church family. You too may be, temporarily at least, stunned by grief. You too will be filled with your own regrets, your own sorrows, and your own questions. You will stand there, by the casket, and watch one person after another break down. And you will feel it every time. Then you will stand there when the casket is closed, one last time.

Suffice to say, this will not be easy. But God has called you, and His Spirit fills you, and others have mentored you, and your people are praying for you, and this family needs you. Jesus blesses those who mourn, and promises that they will be comforted. And He has placed you there, in the midst of broken things, to point people toward comfort of the Healer, the 'Resurrection and the Life" (John 11:25).

RESPONSE TO: THE CASKET

By: Andy McQuitty

Larry's enumeration of the various Funeral Committee roles strikes me as a simple but powerful definition of the word "Pastor." Look at them again with that in mind and see if you don't agree: *Community Organizer, God's Receptionist, Confessor, Journalist, Theologian, Master of Ceremonies, and Open-Air Preacher.*

As pastors, we are called upon to do all of those roles in an ongoing variety of contexts from week to week. What makes conducting a funeral special is that task's demand that we fill all those roles *simultaneously*. When the funeral call comes, we must morph from an individual bit-player into a full-blown Hydra-headed multi-personality "Funeral Committee". That's a scary thought for most of us (and a scary mental image for us all!).

It's almost like an ongoing ministry proficiency exam that pops out of the woodwork on unsuspecting pastors who already don't have enough time left in the week to get their sermon done. Then suddenly they also have to manage a stress-filled, high-stakes funeral service on top of it all. To pull the funeral service off well, you will have to draw on everything you've learned as a theologian and every people-skill you've developed as a minister. Hence, the funeral is the ultimate pop-quiz for pastors, the periodic "check-ride" that objectively demonstrates if we still have the right things going on in our hearts and heads as we captain this latest flight of ministry.

Even so, I find funerals (along with weddings) the most blessed, privileged, and precious things I get to do as a pastor. Sure, they're tough, but they're also amazingly rewarding. Sure, they not only require regular maintenance of our fundamental pastoral skills, but they also require a spiritual tune-up of our hearts and a healthy re-alignment with Heaven's priorities. But when you think of our privilege as pastors to be invited into the center of a family's grief to share this most tender moment in their life and walk with them in it, it makes all the fuss and bother eminently worth it. Who else but a pastor gets such an amazing poignant entre into a major event in a family's never-to-be-forgotten history? I'm always stunned by this privilege people so open-heartedly confer. I'm sure I always will be, too.

Thomas Lynch is an undertaker and writer (how 'bout that combination?) who captures the wonder of a pastor's "Funeral Committee" role when he writes:

"Faith is for the heartbroken, the embittered, the doubting, and the dead. And funerals are the venues at which such folks gather. Some among the clergy have learned to like it. Thus they present themselves at funerals with a good cheer and an unambiguous sympathy that would seem like duplicity in anyone other than a person of faith. I count among the great blessings of my calling that I have known men and women of such bold faith, such powerful witness, that they stand upright between the dead and the living and say, 'Behold I tell you a mystery. . .'"[2]

Getting to do that is more than enough motivation for me to morph into funeral committee mode when the call comes. Yes, it does feel like yet another pastoral pop-quiz. But I know it's that and ever so much more. It's a chance to fulfill my pastoral calling by putting together a service in which I can stand between the dead and the living

---

[2] Thomas Lynch, *The Undertaking* (W. W. Norton & Company 2009). 81

and speak the precious promises of God. For that privilege and joy, I'm even willing to become a community organizer.

And that reminds me. There's one more Funeral Committee role that Larry forgot to list: On the Spot Liturgical Copywriter. It surprises me that he did not list this role as it is one that he himself fills so admirably! Here's my proof. Once Larry and I jointly officiated a funeral at his church for an attendee of my church (it's a long story). Just before the packed service, a grieving family member (who, by virtue of their grief has the divine right to change or add to the service at will) announced that they'd changed the conclusion of the service to a huge balloon release that the preaching pastor (me) would facilitate outside. Alrighty then! As Larry and I turned into the sanctuary to start the service he got a smile on his face and asked, "How are you fixed right about now for balloon-release liturgies?" I rolled my eyes and said no worries, I'll make it up on the fly (no pun intended). Thirty minutes later as we are walking outside for the balloon release, Larry hands me the following note he had hand-scribbled while I preached:

"THIS IS <u>ONLY</u> IF YOU HAVEN'T COME UP WITH A BALOON LITURGY YET.

1. Clouds and Rain—appropriate for what we feel today (it was rainy that day)
2. But if we could get to a higher altitude, the view would look remarkably different—clear and sun and light ("eyes of faith"—higher altitude)
3. Let's let these balloons represent our prayers of faith—that all is not gloom and clouds and rain
4. So now we release prayers of thanksgiving for _____ and resurrection hopes in seeing her again…"

I took that note, cribbed its contents, and walked outside to shamelessly lead that balloon release to the ooh's and aah's of the multitudes. They were taken by the profound depth and beauty of the pastor's spontaneous (and very recently purloined) meditations on the spiritual meaning of letting colorful rubber globes float free to Heaven. So thanks Larry for adding "On the Spot Liturgical Copy-Writer" to your Funeral Committee that day! Not only did you give us all a fine new "balloon liturgy"; you also kept a brother (me!) from crashing and burning which, I think we all agree is never a good thing to do at a funeral.

5

HOT-RIVET SYNDROME

SIGN: THE TIMELY TURNABOUT

By Andy McQuitty

Picture a scene from the Old West, sometime in the 1870's. Weary cowboys in dusty Levi's gather around a blazing campfire after a day in the saddle on the open range. The lonely howl of a coyote counterpoints the muted notes of a guitar as the moon floats serenely overhead. (Eyelids getting heavy?)

Suddenly a bellow of pain shatters the night. A formerly chill cowpoke leaps up and away from the fire, dancing and hooting in agony. Yes, my friends, you know this can only mean one thing: the dreaded "Hot-Rivet Syndrome" has claimed another victim!

In those days, Levi's were made (as they had been from the first days of Levi Strauss) with copper rivets at the jeans' stress points to provide extra strength. On these original Levi's—model 501—the crotch rivet was the critical one. When cowboys crouched too long beside the campfire, the rivet grew uncomfortably hot in that particularly vulnerable place. For years the brave men of the West suffered this curious occupational hazard and many forever walked crooked as a result.

Then in 1933, Walter Haas, Sr., president of Levi Strauss, went camping in his Levi 501's. He was crouched by a crackling campfire in the High Sierras, drinking in the pure mountain air, when he himself fell prey to Hot-Rivet Syndrome. He consulted with professional wranglers in his party. Had they suffered the same mishap? An impassioned YES was the reply! Haas vowed that the offending rivet must go, and at their next meeting, the Levi's board of directors voted it into extinction.[3]

HOT RIVETS AND PROCRASTINATION

The Hot-Rivet Syndrome and its cure are embedded with an important Hobo sign: Make timely turnabouts! An alternate way of saying this might be: "Don't put off making needed changes (no matter how painful they may be) because the pain (and embarrassment) of procrastination will, no doubt, be worse in the long run.

Issac Newton's First Law of Motion states: Everything continues in a state of rest unless it is compelled to change by forces impressed upon it. That's surely true of most people, pastors and Christian leaders included. Some will take the initiative to do what needs doing when they see the light. Others, like Walter Haas, Sr., do what needs doing only when they feel the heat. But how much better is it to do what needs doing expeditiously, not desperately! It may be a pain to

[3] Moskowitz M., M. Katz, and R. Levering, *Everybody's Business: An Almanac: The Irreverent Guide to Corporate America* (Harper & Row 1980)

mess with rivets, but it's a bigger pain to mess with rivets that, due to neglect, get *really hot*.

This is a truism that unfortunately remains largely ignored by half of any given group of people. As Professor Howard Hendricks noted years ago:[4]

1. Early innovators (2.6%), run with new ideas
2. Early adaptors (13.4%), influenced by innovators but not initiators
3. Slow Majority (34%), the herd-followers
4. Reluctant Majority (34%)
5. Antagonistic (16%), they will never change

Painfully, these stats apply not just to rank and file, but head poohbah's as well. It seems that even leaders often choose the procrastination risk of Hot-Rivet Syndrome over doing *now* what will forestall that dreaded condition. The irony is that leaders often do this, not because they are cautious, but because they are procrastinators; not because they are undecided or conflicted, but because they're lazy or afraid.

No wonder Mr. Cumford came up with Cumford's Law (and its corollary): "Nothing is ever done until everyone is convinced that it ought to be done and has been convinced for so long that it is now time to do something else. Corollary: Nothing should ever be done for the first time."

Sadly, many church leaders subscribe to Cumford's Law through procrastination and therefore delay needed "turnabouts". The inevitable result is that they (and their organization) become afflicted with

---

[4] Howard Hendricks, *The Monday Morning Mission* (Wichita KS: Harvest Communications 1984)

Hot-Rivet Syndrome. How do I know this? Because I have been in that group of lazy and scared church leaders off and on for over thirty years and I sport the hot rivet marks to prove it.

As Christian leaders, we need to live our lives as effectively for Jesus and His Kingdom as we possibly can because our time is relatively short on this planet. Because of the responsibilities of our position, we must lead or get out of the way. Leading requires us to be early innovators and adaptors to change, not its antagonistic enemies. And change by definition entails fighting procrastination, which is the formula for status quo.

THE ILLOGIC OF PROCRASTINATION

I believe we leaders procrastinate making needed turnabouts because they are usually painful, or difficult, or both. The result is that our leadership is stymied and our organization suffers. Yet sadly, we often don't connect these dots, choosing instead to make excuses for avoiding painful and difficult (and necessary) changes to provide cover for inaction.

But no, time alone doesn't make everything better, because bad news doesn't automatically get better with time. Also, hard tasks don't get easier with time, and painful conversations don't become more pleasant with time. In fact, all these rivets just get hotter with time! So why not jump out of the jeans sooner rather than later? It just makes sense to be proactive especially since, in the long run, it's surely less painful.

HOT RIVETS TO AVOID

By its very nature, good leadership regularly births new rivets. Leadership means change, and change means action, and action often is arduous. If we are not willing to take action regarding the hard and painful things that naturally flow from change, they will become hot rivets that burn us later. So, it's face the music now or feel the heat later! Here are a few examples of the kinds of rivets that procrastination makes hot:

- That conversation with an opinion leader in your organization who has not bought into your vision for the future. (She's not going to put a lid on this of her own volition but continue to undermine you if unchecked). Make the call. *Now.*
- Letting go of a staffer who is in over his head and is single-handedly dragging your whole team down. His incompetence won't get better with time. Set the severance process in motion. Make the appointment. *Now.*
- That position paper you need to write to get your board and staff on the same page on a controversial issue. You know it is going to be a tricky, arduous, time-consuming albeit vital task. Open a new doc and get to work. *Now.*
- That new personal spiritual disciplines' regimen that you know your cold heart needs to get you reconnected to the anchor of your soul. Begin today. No, check that. . . *now.*
- That note of condolence, that letter of recognition, that email of connection that you need to write to nurture vital relationships in your leadership network. Write it *now.*
- That engagement you need to schedule even though your calendar is packed and all you want to do is find a window for a measly day off. Book it *now.*

- That new filing system that is going to aid your ministry for decades to come if only it ever gets created? Go to Office Max today. (in this case *now* might be a bit over-the-top!).
- That ministry vision revamp you've been mulling over for years because you know your team needs motivation and focus. Get a date on the calendar and start the journey together ... today (see the parenthetical above).

The beauty of beating procrastination in ministry is that a leader can become virtually free from all fear of hot rivets. Becoming procrastination free most certainly does not preclude all problems. These we will, along with the poor, have always with us. But becoming procrastination-free does ease our mind from the looming menace of hot rivets, and that's a good thing. So kick back, build a great big camp fire and put on s'mores without a second thought. And do it *now*.

RESPONSE TO:
THE TIMELY TURNABOUT

By: Larry Parsley

Ouch. This essay hit me right where it hurts the most! If I didn't know better, I would think that Pastor Andy has been working for the N.S.A., monitoring my email and calendar and meetings with staff members.

This essay made me painfully aware that I am a shepherd who (along with my sheep) shares a general aversion to change. And sometimes it is hard for me to know whether laziness or fear is the bigger driver. Sometimes I hear pastor friends describe a season where they are entering a capital campaign. They will be in the middle of a grueling gauntlet of meetings—perhaps multiple dinners each night, 5-6 days a week. And still, they must write sermons and supervise staff and care for the sheep. And I think to myself: "That's too much work. Who would willingly sign up for that?" That's laziness talking. Sabbath is a divine discipline, but so is suffering. Sometimes a demanding leadership regimen is the path to moving the church forward.

But fear is usually the larger driver for me. In the presidential election of 1980, Ronald Reagan won by a "landslide" (while claiming almost 59% of the popular vote). While for Mr. Reagan, 59% of the popular vote is a landslide, in the pastoral life, it only takes those 10% of "antagonists to change" to cause major grief. Churches are often driven (by practicality, if not by polity) by a bias for consensus. We do not want to move forward on an issue until everybody's thumb points toward the ceiling. Even those who agree with change will vote against it if a good friend's thumb points toward the ground.

Given my predilections toward laziness and fear, I need these challenging words. The rivets will not get cooler. Problems in ministry generally do not solve themselves. The way *out* of this current circumstance is the way *through*. And for the sake of sensitivities, the sooner the better!

6

MARRIAGE COUNSELING IS WAR

SIGN: THE BATTLEFIELD

By: Larry Parsley

When I do marriage counseling, I go to war. I know that may sound melodramatic, but that's what it feels like—warfare. Why war?

It is war because no border or boundary is sacred.

Whether it is your looks, your weight, your hygiene, your mother, your sexual prowess (or lack thereof), nothing is spared from critique.

IT IS WAR BECAUSE FEW WEAPONS ARE OFF-LIMITS.

Profanity, bitterness, stonewalling, physical aggression, toxic sarcasm, rehearsing the worst mistakes another has made, or holding their weaknesses and deficits against them. Too often, when couples fight, they fight to win. And if they can get off a sucker punch, they will.

IT IS WAR BECAUSE OF THE IMPORTANCE OF THE ELEMENT OF SURPRISE

Spouses will plan for weeks, months, or even years to execute that decisive act of treachery against their wedding vows. And then it's Pearl Harbor for the unsuspecting spouse.

IT IS WAR BECAUSE THE WOUNDS ARE BRUTAL TO BEHOLD.

She stops eating: she can't sleep. He's usually a stoic, but he can't seem to stop crying. She can't stay home with the kids anymore, though that's her vocation (indeed, her calling). He can't kiss his kids goodnight every night anymore.

IT IS WAR BECAUSE INNOCENT CIVILIANS ARE AFFECTED.

That little boy didn't do anything to contribute to the end of this marriage, but in his heart, he believes it is his fault. He thinks that if he had kept his room cleaner, or not talked back as much or fought with his sister, somehow that would have created a happier environment in the home, and mommy and daddy would still be together. It is not his fault, but he may think it is.

My daughter loves to steal a hug. If she catches me hugging her mom, she can't wait to wrap her little arms around both of us. That's what every child wants, whether she can verbalize it or not. She wants to be able to wrap her arms around an organism: Mom-and-Dad. Children don't want to have to worry about loyalty to mom being disloyalty to dad. They don't want to pack a suitcase just to spend the night with a parent. They don't want two sets of parents lighting one side of the unity candle at their wedding. They don't want to be in two different homes on Christmas day. They don't want to have to worry about making step-parents and step-siblings 'feel right at home' (whatever that means).

IT IS WAR BECAUSE OF COLLATERAL DAMAGE.

Houses get sold, businesses get dissolved, and a church likely loses custody of one spouse or another. And often, my mere identity as a pastor makes me the bad guy, and church members whom I thought of as friends stop returning my calls.

I've never been to war, so I don't have a right to say it. But I'm telling you, it feels like war. So, I go to war.

BUT IN ALL HONESTY, I'M NOT ALWAYS SURE WHERE I AM SHOOTING.

Sometimes I want to fire off a few rounds of righteous retribution at the wife who withheld sex from her husband for a year. How could she not know what that would do to the man? Or I want to lob a holy grenade at the husband, who checked out emotionally from his marriage long ago. *Did you really think she would want to stay married to a zombie? Did you really think your paycheck was all she needed?* Or sometimes I'd like to track down the parents of these two spouses. *You contributed to their brokenness. You failed to give them viable role models for how to live.*

And frequently, too frequently in times of marital brokenness in the church, I want to turn my wrath upon myself. I am angry with me, for aiding and abetting a superficial church culture, where people were free to discuss the weather and the soccer tournament and the window treatments and deer blinds, and even the difference between different Greek words for "love," but they apparently never felt free to discuss the relational hell that was burning down their own homes. And I have to stare down from the pulpit on a Sunday morning at those three little kids—days after a parent moves out of the house—and I think: "I failed them." Or at the very least, I didn't do enough to protect them. So, I go to war.

AND WHEN I CLEAR MY HEAD, I GO TO WAR WITH THE EVIL ONE.

The apostle Paul said it well in Ephesians 6:12: "*For our struggle is not against flesh and blood, but against the rulers, against the authorities, against the powers of this dark world and against the spiritual forces of evil in the heavenly realms.*" Our struggle is not with flesh and blood, not with him or her or their parents or their pastor. Our battle, our war as pastors, is with the forces of darkness that continually grab a crowbar and pry apart what 'God hath joined together.' It is only the Evil One who could bring about this much pain and suffering and destruction.

I have had divorced people describe to me different kinds of pain they've endured in their lives, and then tell me that, in the hierarchy of pain, divorce is at the top. *Nothing hurts like this hurts*, they say. Only the Evil One could dream up a disruption like marital brokenness, whose destructive power creates aftershocks through the generations. To paraphrase the prophet Jeremiah (31:29), their fathers and mothers ate the sour grapes of divorce, and the 'children's teeth are set on edge.' Only the Evil One could spend so much time fueling the scandal of the Evangelical church—we who believe the Bible, we who believe the gospel, and yet who routinely accept divorce as inevitable and, in some cases, even healthy. What a scandal! A broken marriage is a contradiction of the gospel.

A broken marriage denies everything the gospel affirms. The gospel says that our sins can be forgiven. But a broken marriage says that the weight of grievances against one another is too much. The gospel says that we can change, but divorce is built on the premise that people can't change. The gospel calls on us as beneficiaries of the cross to take up our own crosses and follow Jesus, but divorce is built on the premise that suffering is not worth it. The gospel is all about 'eucatastrophe,' to use Tolkien's phrase, about certain disaster averted, about resurrection Sundays that follow dark Good Friday's. But divorce is ever and only about plain old, garden-variety 'catastrophe' with no "eu" but only dark Good Friday's in sight.

Too often, we pastors have colluded with the Evil One to preach a truncated gospel (which is no gospel at all). We've said to the one leaving, 'go back.' And that's all we've said. *Go back to Marriage 1.0. Divorce is wrong, so go back and live in hell for the next 40 years.* We've given them law, and really only a part of the law, only a fraction of the Scripture. The Bible says a lot more about marriage and divorce than simply that God hates divorce (Malachi 2:16).

In my experience, the one who separates is often the most aggrieved party. To address them solely, and to do nothing more than send them back to Marriage 1.0, is to perform pastoral malpractice. It is to offer the hurting only law, but no grace or hope. We've got to speak the whole truth of Scripture and grace to both, even if one party is not a Christian. This might be our grand opening. Unbelieving spouses may not want Jesus, but they often *do* want their marriage to stay viable. And if they figure out that Jesus can help them restore their marriage, they may do more than just *use* Jesus. They may be brought to their knees before His cross.

AND SO, WHEN I GO TO DO MARRIAGE COUNSELING, I GO TO WAR.

I climb into a bomber plane and drop prayer after prayer after prayer on the target. I pray for providential events that move couples toward one another and not away from one another. I pray for that reconciliation muscle, no matter how small, to exercise itself. I pray for shafts of sunlight to sneak into dungeons of despair.

AND THEN I MARSHAL THE INFANTRY.

Church leaders and small group leaders and fellow staff members and myself are called to inhabit the trenches. We use emails and phone calls and texts and shared coffee at Starbucks as a means of advocating for the marriage and for reconciliation.

AND OFTEN, I ENGAGE IN HAND-TO-HAND COMBAT

Hand-to-hand combat requires the weapons of 'sword of the spirit' and 'praying in the Spirit' (Ephesians 6). Not too long ago I was engaged in premarital counseling, but it felt like post-marital counseling. This couple would verbally brutalize one another in front of me during our counseling sessions, and at the end of the session I would tell them, "I can't marry you, because I don't marry enemies." They would return to me the next day: contrite, prayerful, apologetic. "Pastor, we've prayed, and we're ready to go forward." And I, full of hope, would start over with them again.

And then the same said pattern would recur. It happened all the way up to the wedding weekend, complete with a peacemaking conversation minutes before the wedding rehearsal was to begin. It happened when I called the family the morning of the wedding to a mandatory meeting, where I walked through Colossians 3, verse-by-verse, addressing words to each family member present. I hoped and prayed for their reconciliation, but what we ended up with was a cancelled wedding. That cancellation, as painful as it was, trumped a miserable marriage.

I GO TO WAR, LEADING THE CORPS OF ENGINEERS TO BUILD 'FIELD HOSPITALS'

I read an article a few years ago in <u>Newsweek</u> about an American urologist named Richard Jadick.[5] He was living a pretty comfortable life in Georgia when he became burdened about the shortage of medical doctors in the war in Iraq. So, with his wife nine months pregnant with their first child, he made the decision to go to Fallujah. And his decision was strongly influenced by something that battlefield surgeons refer to as the "golden hour." A badly injured person has a better chance of survival if they can get to a hospital within <u>one hour</u>. But in this field of conflict, helicopter evacuations are often out of the question. So Jadick made a decision: instead of bringing the soldiers to the doctors, he himself would go to the soldiers.

Churches must reclaim the 'golden hour.' We have to build field hospitals in our ministries, training leaders to spot signs of dysfunctional marriages. We point people toward marriage enrichment small groups and retreat experiences. We lovingly challenge people to disclose what is broken in their marriages. We must remember that in the battlefield of marriage, time is of the essence.

AND TOO OFTEN, WHEN I GO TO WAR, I LOSE.

I watch couples, who for 5 or 10 or 20 or 30 years have daily built walls of separation. And now that wall becomes a stronghold that

---

[5] "On Call in Hell," Pat Wingert, Newsweek, March 2006.

neither one is able or willing to find the spiritual resources to knock down. Sometimes, praise God, walls are knocked down and couples are reunited.

But not often.

Still, I go to war. What else can a pastor do?

RESPONSE TO: THE BATTLEFIELD

By: Andy McQuitty

Tears rolled down my cheeks when Larry described the wounded children of spousal combatants as "innocent civilians". Over the years, I've also comforted that little boy who wrongly believes his parents' divorce was his fault and hugged that distraught little girl who can no longer "wrap her little arms around an organism, Mom-and-Dad, Inc.". Add to that the brutal emotional wounds and real-life collateral damage inflicted upon the lives of the parental former spouses, and I conclude there's just nothing more heartbreaking for parents and children in this world (not to mention their pastors) than having their family torn apart by divorce!

So yes, I heartily agree with Larry when he uses a metaphor (*not* a simile!) in declaring, "marriage counseling is war". It's not "like" war (simile). It *is* war (metaphor). It's not a benign meeting of minds that makes much of sympathizing and excuse-making and offering helpful suggestions often designed (unfortunately) to equip families for "soft landings". Rather, it *is* a full-on spiritual, special forces operation undertaken by warring spouses and directed by their Battlefield Chaplain!

I insist that this "Operation Reconciliation" must be undertaken by the warring spouses themselves because they--not their pastor or counsellor or lawyer or friends--are the only ones who can do the hard spiritual and emotional work to win the battle! Early on, I was flattered when an angry or hurt husband or wife invited me as their pastor to be a knight-in-shining-armor and "save" their marriage (which was by then almost in divorce court). Then I began to suspect that I was actually being hornswoggled into becoming the sacrificial lamb upon whose inadequate efforts the marriage failure could be blamed, thus granting plausible deniability to one or both spouses of saying, "at least we tried". Nope. Not really!

So my Hobo friends, here's the first thing you do when the call comes in: have a kind and compassionate but also pointed conversation with each spouse in which you express your willingness to help them let God heal their marriage, but only if both declare their heartfelt desire to reconcile (even if they don't see how that's possible) as well as their willingness to do the hard emotional and spiritual work that reconciliation requires.

You will lead and direct them over coming months of counselling sessions, but *they* must do the work with the empowerment of the Holy Spirit. If they're unwilling or unmotivated to do so, your counselling ministry sadly must become a ministry of consolation. But assuming that spouses in conflict are willing to fight for their marriage, the Battlefield Chaplain (you) steps boldly into their fog of war with two clear tactical objectives for each one:

1. **Genuine Repentance**

   Each spouse acknowledging how they have sinned against their mate and then repenting for that sin constitutes the first glimmer of hope for the marriage. But it must be genuine repentance and not just a smokescreen designed to save face. It must consist of true sorrow for their sin and not just for themselves. As Tim Keller observes:

"True repentance begins where whitewashing ("Nothing really happened") and blame shifting ("I'm sorry, but you know it really wasn't my fault") and self - pity ("I'm sorry because of what it has cost me") and self-flagellation ("I will feel so terrible no one will be able to criticize me") end. . . Here is the language of a repentant heart : "Yes, Lord, I have been mistreated, and I've had troubles, but I did not react to these conditions as I should have. It is my own sin that is the reason I am miserable today. I take full responsibility!" Repentance begins where blame shifting ends" (Tim Keller, *Forgive: Why Should I, How Can I?* Viking Press, p. 149).

2. **Full Forgiveness**

The Battlefield Chaplain's next tactical objective for warring spouses after genuine repentance is full forgiveness. This essential step closes the loop on reconciliation and begins the healing process. Again, Tim Keller tells us why full forgiveness is so important. "Unless you forgive deliberately, thoroughly, and with all the help Christ offers, your anger will "defile" you, as Hebrews says. . .wrath can make you a wraith, turning you slowly but surely into a restless spirit, into someone who's controlled by the past, someone who's haunted (Tim Keller, *Forgive: Why Should I, How Can I?*, Viking Press, p. 163).

The stakes are extremely high for a pastor who ventures into marriage counseling, not to mention for the warring spouses who are being counselled. That's why Larry started this chapter with his stunning metaphor: "When I do marriage counseling, I go to war." All of us pastors become Battlefield Chaplains when we gladly jump into the fray of a wounded marriage bearing faith, hope, and love. Nothing is harder. But for happy, grace-filled warriors, nothing is more worth it either!

7

GOD IS NOT YOUR PR AGENT

SIGN: THE TOTEM POLE

By: Andy McQuitty

We've all been there. Conferences or local pastoral gatherings where the men of the cloth schmooze before and after sessions with the subconscious agenda of defining where everyone ranks on the success totem pole.

Now lower those eyebrows. You know it's true.

It's bad form of course to come right out and ask a new acquaintance how big his church is. Over-eagerness to discover one's place in the pecking order betrays a needy sense of insecurity and low self-esteem. Don't humiliate yourself by letting on you want to know what you know everyone else wants to know too!

No, you learn to get at the vital information by more subtle means. Ask a few questions about denominational affiliations, worship style, common friends and associates and you just might glean the useful information that you seek. "Yeah, when we started that contemporary service, it immediately doubled the 300 we had in attendance at the traditional." Voilà. Now you know they're running 900 and if you're at 1900,the you've got this guy beat whether he knows it or not. And so on.

What is it with preachers that they seem driven to know this stuff? (Notice how I went to the third person when raising this convicting question). I believe the answer lies in two insidious misapprehensions that result in a devastatingly debilitating and common pastoral sin. Thus, the hobo warning sign I'd like to offer pastors is this: the totem pole. As in, God is not your PR Agent, so stop asking him to move you up the ministry totem pole!

SUCCESS: THE FINAL FRONTIER

The first serious misapprehension of pastors is that success in ministry is somehow defined by nickels and noses. Obviously, it is not. But we're tempted to see it that way because nickels and noses are so much more conveniently measurable than true spiritual growth in our congregations. So by all means, let's count!

Now I'm not averse to counting, nor do I think a church that is growing in numbers is a bad thing. What I'm challenging is the idea that big equals success. It may. Or it may not. We've all seen churches pull tricks out of the gimmick box and triple their attendance. So what? That may look good to us, but smell bad to God.

On the other hand, we've all seen faithful pastors here and on foreign soil laboring for the Kingdom only to be rewarded with dwindling congregations. That may look bad but be a sweet savor in the halls of Heaven.

Growing numbers in a church are most often a good thing but sometimes can be a bad thing. What's essential is that we not automatically equate them to success. Neither is success automatically measured by the size of your church facilities, or the amount you're spending on the new building project, or how much money you have in the bank, or how many books you have in print, or how many times you've delivered the invocation at City Council Meetings, or whether you've got a couple of lines in Who's Who of America.

Those things are all fine, but can we all go back for a moment to those halcyon days of our idealistic pastoral youth when we saw success in terms of faithfulness? When teaching truth, and ministering to the struggling, and loving God and others well, and finishing strong were our goals? Can we go back to when we were willing to just serve and leave the size and scope of our "career" to God? As no less a light than J.I. Packer wrote: "Faithfulness, godliness, and loving service are the divine measure of real success in ministry"[6]

If Dr. Packer was right (and what mere mortal has the temerity to claim otherwise?), then "God as my PR agent" thinking flies in the face of true success for us as pastors. It exalts external results while God celebrates quiet perseverance.

At the beginning of the megachurch age some years ago, who can forget Mother Teresa's startling pronouncement: "I do not pray for success, I ask for faithfulness." To her, faithfulness equaled success. She also famously said, "We can do no great things, only small things with great love." Note the emphasis here on how and why ministers do what they do, not on the results of what ministers do. When we turn our focus from faithfulness to results, it's a short hop and skip

6 J. I. Packer, *Christiantiy Today*, August 12, 1988, https://www.christianitytoday.com/, 15

to appropriating God as our PR Agent: "I'm God's servant and I just know He wants me to look good by giving me impressive ministry results that I can talk (brag) about with other pastors at conference breaks. God is so good!"

WHAT GOD OWES PASTORS

If you choked on that subtitle, good. (If you didn't, I'm really glad you're reading this chapter). Pastors who wrongly define ministry success have a big problem: the false expectation planted in their psyches that God's faithfulness assures them a big, impressive ministry. Nobody enters any vocation wanting to fail, pastors included. In fact, pastors have some biblical encouragement to believe that God will give them "good success" if they are faithful in their service. But if the definition of that success is unbiblical, we pastors logically conclude that God owes us growing churches with healthy budgets and expanding influence.

The unwritten "success" contract we strike with God goes something like this. "Lord, I'll serve you faithfully, preach passionately, lead wisely, and pray consistently, and in return we both know (wink, wink) that even though you never promised I'd have an outwardly impressive, growing church, I will. Because I owe you certain things in my role as pastor and promise to fulfill them, I'm confident you're aware that, in return, you owe me certain things in your role as God. Thanks Father for this beautiful relationship! I can't wait to move ahead with you as my PR Agent."

Do any of us really think that way? Yes, most of us do, just not consciously or, if we do, we don't admit it even to ourselves. But telltale signs that pastors think God is their PR agent are everywhere.

Show me a pastor who is becoming increasingly cynical about people because of the constant drumbeat of criticism he's receiving, and I'll show you a pastor who thinks God is his PR agent. His cynicism arises not from criticism; that's no surprise even to novice leaders. His cynicism arises from his disappointment that God as PR Agent is falling down on the job. C'mon God, my image needs some burnishing here!

Show me a pastor who becoming increasingly annoyed because people are resisting his leadership or because the church around the corner is growing and his isn't, and I'll show you a pastor who thinks God is his PR agent. His aggravation arises not from slow growth or recalcitrant congregants, but from disappointment that God is breaching his PR Agent contract. I'm doing my part, God, so when are you going to do yours?

Not only is the PR Agent moniker insulting to the Almighty, I also have to think that He gets piqued by pastors assigning Him the blame when their ministry initiatives tank. They're thinking, "God, why aren't you blessing this handy-dandy new program I just launched?" and God is thinking, "That's the most asinine new program I've seen launched in that church for many a year."

Could it be that sometimes we fail, not because God let us down, but because we were unprepared, naïve, brash, or stupid? (I've done many stupid things in ministry over the years and found none of them produced fruit, even though I prayed over them first). One great skill that experience hones is the ability to discern the right message in failure. It's never "God blew it," but often "I'm operating outside the sphere of my giftedness" or "my plan and strategy here needs tweaking" or "maybe I should have secured funding from the Board before I announced the new building project to the congregation." It's the little things that trip us up. As powerful as prayer is, I've found that God rarely allows it to trump incompetence.

While we pastors are getting secretly ticked off at God, what we ought to be doing is seeking out some wise mentors who can help us take an objective look at what's going wrong. There are a million reasons why a given ministry takes off or tanks. Some of those reasons are spiritual. Most are practical. It's attractive to focus on the spiritual reasons for us pastors though, because proclaiming that "Satan is attacking" goes down easier than "my preaching sucks." I'm not saying the former explanation is never applicable, just that the latter one is more likely to be accurate.

IF GOD IS YOUR PR AGENT, YOUR MINISTRY MIGHT JUST BE YOUR GOD (IDOLATRY REVISITED)

The logical negative progression in the life of a pastor of these two misapprehensions—that success can be counted and that "God is my PR Agent"—is insidious. It can lead not only to his discouragement and exit from the ministry, but even to questioning the very existence of the God he once served. And all of this because the pastor in question replaced worshipping God with working for God in the church. When working for God in the church fizzled, so did his faith in God. We have a word for replacing God with anything else—idolatry. Paradoxically enough, idolatry is a besetting pastoral sin which inevitably leads to severe theological disillusionment. After all, if my God has become my ministry and my ministry is doing a swirly, then maybe I can just do without God altogether. I've known some former clergy over the years who became so disillusioned with the false God of ministry success that they ditched the ministry and now live as practical atheists.

Years ago, I, like so many pastors at one point or another, was sorely tempted to ditch the ministry. I was a fresh-faced, newly married college grad about a year into my first ever ministry gig as a youth pastor--and deeply discouraged. 85 percent of the church of 1600 where I served was 65 years of age or older; looking back, it would have been a shrewder move on my part to apply as pastor of geriatrics than youth pastor! Nevertheless, there I was presiding over a (pathetically small) youth group comprised of two high school students and four middle school students. When taking up the position of youth pastor, I was only fifty percent experienced: I had never been a pastor, but had indeed once been a teenager. That was it. My sum total of ministry training was nil, and I wonder to this day why I was ever hired for the position. They must have been desperate. All I knew after that first year was that now I was desperate.

I can sum up why I was tempted to ditch that youth ministry very simply: Nothing I tried worked. My rationale for taking the job with no experience right out of college was threefold. First, only six kids? Even I can't take that any lower! Second, only six kids? I'll have time to learn on the job. And third, only six kids? No worries, God cares about the youth of the city and will help me turn six into six hundred! (Read, "God is my PR Agent")

It took about a year for each of my savvy rationales to crash and burn. Can't take it any lower? I "de—grew" the group from six to four. Time for some OTJ training? No, too much time given to fielding complaints about my bad youth program. God is my PR Agent? Not! I was quite sure, however, that the Almighty was on the side of youth in our city—just not my particular youth ministry. Several other church groups were exploding while I sat fizzling, wondering where

God was in my time of need. I seriously began to look into alternate career opportunities.

But before I threw in the towel, I decided to take a week alone for some rest and reflection (and respite from the unrelenting reminders at church of what a dismal failure I was as a youth pastor). I got away and read Scripture, spent lots of time thinking and praying, and took some fantastic naps.

As I did, I came to a couple of powerful insights. First, God is sovereign and His word was profound and wonderful. This was not a revelation to God, just to a little youth pastor who had subtly stopped looking to His Heavenly Father for encouragement and strength and to "results" in ministry instead. Second, I realized that if my faltering, minuscule youth program never grew or even if it went away, God is still good and I loved Him and owed Him my life in service and could trust His word no matter what. It hit me one day while sitting in a canoe eating a peanut butter cracker, "God is not my PR Agent. I need to stop treating Him like one."

That was a breakthrough for me. I found myself actually enjoying the Word again because I was listening for God's voice and not scouring the sacred text for a clue as to why my junior higher's thought my talks were boring. I found myself loving Jesus again just for who He is and not being secretly peeved that He was blessing that youth pastor down the street with a growing ministry even though I was way more spiritual.

I found it terrifically freeing to acknowledge consciously that, though God had given me all spiritual blessings in the heavenly places, He owed me squat when it came to nickels and noses. His deity and goodness and my response of service and love had nothing whatsoever to do with whether I ever broke the "20" barrier in my high school group's attendance.

When I returned from my little getaway, I found that an amazing stronghold had been smashed in my pastoral heart. I was no longer an idolater. I no longer looked to ministry results to affirm my spirituality and I no longer derived my sense of worthiness as a human being from whether or not I could keep ninth graders from smoking pot on church grounds.

I guess you could say I stopped the unhealthy practice of worshipping my ministry, and resumed the very healthy for all pastors' practice of worshipping only God once again.

Oddly enough, that's actually when that little youth ministry began to turn around—when I stopped insisting that God turn it around to make me look good. Sure, I implemented a new game plan and partnered with some other great youth leaders in the city and got some mentoring to figure out where I was making my most egregious errors in programming, and that helped. But I have to think that the main reason things looked up was that God was pleased that I was eschewing idolatry and no longer treating him like my PR Agent genii-in-the-bottle.

I find that I have to de-idolatrize my heart fairly frequently as a pastor by just chopping that totem pole right down (especially after attending conferences). But I'm quite confident that God is pleased by the practice and I highly recommend it to you, my fellow pastors!

RESPONSE TO:
THE TOTEM POLE

By: Larry Parsley

There is a good reason why many of us do not like to go see a physician. Physicians have a way of getting 'up close and personal' with us about those aspects of our lives which are unwell. Sometimes, the very presence of something out of whack in our physical bodies is, in fact, a *disincentive* to go see a doctor. *After all, if I show up for the appointment, the doc might discover that something is truly wrong with me. Then what would I do?*

I could not help but feel similarly as I read Andy's chapter. I don't know about you, but I felt Dr. Andy poking around at places in my pastoral psyche that I would much rather be left untouched. "Does this hurt?" *Yes, now leave it alone, please!*

Too often, we pastors are like salespeople and shortstops—obsessed with our statistics, and fiercely competitive. While that competition might push success on the field or at the salesmanship club, it will not have the same effect upon those of us who have taken up crosses. Instead, our godly motivation will be replaced by a craven need to be seen as the most successful pastor around. And when our version of success fails to materialize, as Andy succinctly points out, we will turn our anger upon the very God who is trying to teach us a different way.

Most pastors do not need Balaam to prove that our sermons can be orthodox while our hearts are idolatrous. We feel it deep inside our sin-sick souls. But sometimes, God allows the collapse of numerical indicators of ministry success (as Andy narrates in his youth ministry remembrances) so that something new can be built in our hearts. And when that happens, as hard as it is at the time, God trades us "beauty" for 'ashes" (Isaiah 61:3).

8

HIRING NEW STAFF: GETTING IT RIGHT THE FIRST TIME

THE SIGN: THE ENVELOPE

By Larry Parsley

One of the most significant ways you will either help or hinder your church is by the staff members you hire. Hire well—a called, gifted, healthy, and well-suited minister to your staff—and there's a strong possibility that the new staff member will bless your church for decades. Hire poorly, and you may lose months off your life as you endure their poor leadership and the grief that comes with moving them on.

In my experience, few things are more difficult on a pastorate than a poor staff hire.

So what are some things I look for in a new staff member?

SOMEBODY WHO HAS GOTTEN OVER THEMSELVES

Often a minister's journey toward vocational ministry begins when somebody notices that the embryonic pastor is good at something. Perhaps, they have a beautiful singing voice, or they just seem to be a natural born leader. Perhaps, when they were in high school, they preached on Youth Sunday sermon and didn't do a half-bad job.

So, in the church body, this future minister is elevated among their peers. They are treated as 'extra special,' more special than the other Christians, because God has given them clear gifts. And then they may go through a special degree program at Bible college or seminary, for "special people." And then they arrive at their first church as a small-c celebrity. They begin to be esteemed even more highly. And if the minister is successful, and especially if the church experiences numerical growth under the minister's watch, then their success becomes more well known.

It's an old story, but sometimes the minister can equate their 'success' with their specialness. Forget 'I planted and Apollos waters but God gives the increase' (1 Corinthians 3:6) No, the increase is inextricably linked with the wonderfulness of the minister!

Now, in the lives of most ministers, God is especially merciful to allow that minister to experience abject failure, as a way of teaching them that they are not the key variable. Some have not been so blessed with that lesson and instead deflect their ministry setbacks on laypeople who 'don't get it' or the elders or the deacons or the lame staff members around them.

I want to hire somebody who has learned that lesson: who has gotten over themselves. I'd really like to hire someone who has experienced a little bit of failure. Let me qualify that. I'm not talking about moral failure or apostasy, to be sure. I'm talking about a failure that results in someone who knows that ministry is about a lot more than their charismatic personality and their cool haircut. Such failure leads to humility, and wisdom, and a deeper dependence upon the God who truly 'gives the increase.'

THE 'EYE OF THE TIGER'

I am always on the lookout for a future staff member who feels an unmistakable call of God to come to my church. In other words, I am searching for a person who, for this run in their life, believe that they were born to do 'this job.'

I've interviewed people before who could *do* the job description (in other words, they had the necessary skills and the requisite education). But perhaps they are trying to get out of a bad situation. Maybe they are living in a state of vocational confusion: they are open to doing many different roles, but not sure they can land on just one. I feel for that person … I really do! But I don't want them on my staff.

You see, there are so many obstacles in ministry that will threaten to slow you down. And one of the things that propels a staff member is a clear, clarion call—not just to vocational ministry in general, but to the current role we're advertising.

INTERNALLY MOTIVATED

I'd much rather find a staff member working late and tell them to go home, than a staff member who routinely comes in late and you have to call them to see where they are. I don't look for a workaholic, but I do look for a hard worker.

I realize that I write these words in an era that wisely focuses on Sabbath and self-care and work-life balance. All of these are good things. The minister has to battle the chaos of overflowing task lists and impossible expectations. I'm not looking for a person who does not know her limits. I'm not fond of the Messiah complex. Yes, rest and renewal are vital.

At the same time, when we are called to serve, we are called to suffer. If we don't have some sleepless nights and fatigued days that are directly connected to our ministry, we are likely doing it wrong.

So I want the staff member working for me who truly 'works for the Lord' (and whose work ethic reveals it).

TRUTH-SPEAKER: FILLED WITH COURAGE *AND* SELF-CONTROL

I look for someone with the courage to speak the painful truth to me, but enough self-control not to speak the painful truth about me to others. I want, and need, a staff member who can look me in the eye and speak the unadorned truth I need to hear. I need to know when constituencies are upset, when job expectations are out of whack, when the vision is leaking, or when our team is demotivated. I'd love for the staff member to say it with gentleness and diplomacy, but above all I need them to say it.

But I need them to say it to me. I learned this from my first pastor, who told me, "Larry, you can say anything you want to me if you say it in love. But don't let me find out you're saying it about me out there. Because that's not loving."

NOT A 'CHERRY-PICKER'

I fear the staff member who only wants to do eat the cherries and ice cream of ministry, but not the green beans and lima beans and spinach of ministry. It is one thing to work out of our giftedness; it is quite another to assume that there won't be anything hard or painful in our job description.

Sometimes, new staff members balk at carrying on a predecessor's program. And yes, sometimes old programs need to be allowed to retire. Sometimes.

At other times, a traditional ministry has really caught fire with the congregation. There's a sense of momentum as parishioners look forward to the annual launch of this particular program. I need a staff member who will is humble enough to build upon a predecessor's work, to honor healthy traditions, and to renew them and keep them alive for the next generation. This will require a willingness to embrace the job description the church needs, and not necessarily the special things a staff member most loves doing.

LONG TENURES

Yes, every pastor knows that God is the boss, and we must be willing to go even to Ninevah if God wills it. It is a little foolhardy to announce to a congregation that you will retire with them. At the same time, however, I get a little concerned when a resume shows many short tenures linked together.

Short tenures tell me that the staff member is likely impatient and cannot fight through adversity, or that they don't know how to work with leaders, or that they are ambitiously jumping ship and building their own careers at the expense of the churches they leave behind.

You will likely sink a tremendous amount of time into a thorough staff search, and you'd like to think that your effort will result in a new staff member's longevity.

PLAYS BY THE RULES OF THE SEARCH

When we have a job opening, we frequently post it on a number of different ministry websites, as well as engaging in our own networking. When we do post a position, the wording is very clear about the person on our staff who is responsible for receiving the resumes (and generally it's not me … I'm not that administratively savvy to handle all that paper and email).

But invariably, when a job is posted, applicants will go to our church's website, find my name and email address, and they'll send their resume and cover letter to me.

Early on, I would answer these emails and forward their resumes to our contact person. And then I started to think to myself: "Why am I doing this?" This applicant has just demonstrated that they don't like our process, or that the rules of our process don't apply to them. To me, that behavior makes me generally weary of candidates that come on too strong. I don't mind good, old-fashioned initiative (and even a little bit of chutzpah). But I worry about the candidate who doesn't seem to trust the Holy Spirit and tries to force the issue themselves.

"TELL ME ABOUT YOUR LAST CHURCH"

Sometimes I'll hear a candidate say something like this: "At my last church, the preacher was boring and the administrative assistants were rude and the lay leaders didn't get it and the youth room smelled like mothballs … but I love what I'm seeing at your church."

Now, I know that ministers can find themselves in really difficult church situations—that they can be misled by search committees, and that the number one song on their mind is that great hymn, "Please Release Me, Let Me Go."

But generally speaking, I am looking for the staff member that has something good to say about the church they're leaving. It's not an absolute truth, but I think that more often than not, people that have a miserable time at Church A and a miserable time at Church B will likely have a miserable time at your church. Why? Because they bring their negative attitude with them wherever they go.

BLESSED BY A HEALTHY FAMILY

Some of us are old enough to remember the days when a staff member (usually male) was interviewed *with* his wife. And the thinking of many old school search committees was this: "Let's see if we can get two for the price of one." In other words, we'll hire him to be our full-time worship pastor, but we will expect her to play the piano and lead the youth choir and organize the women's retreat and chair the mission's banquet and on and on we go.

We can pray that those days are passing us by. We like to hire 'one for the price of one.'

Still, as pastors, we bring our families to work with us. And I love to hire staff members who belong to healthy families. You are likely very familiar with Paul's words to Timothy in 1 Timothy 3:4–5, which states that a church leader "must manage his own family well and see that his children obey him, and he must do so in a manner worthy of full respect (If anyone does not know how to manage his own family, how can he take care of God's church?)." So, certainly, there is a strong connection between leadership in our houses and leadership in God's house.

Not only that, our families will need to be healthy enough to endure the added scrutiny and pressures which come their way, solely by virtue of being genetically connected to the minister. A healthy family has a built-in immune system to absorb a congregation's toxins and not get sick.

If you get nothing else from this book, you will certainly discover that ministry is hard. Ministers often leave work discouraged by the heaviness of the job, the unrealistic expectations of congregants, the drag of working through relational conflict, and the sting of fair and unfair criticism. But if that staff member can go home to a family that loves them, distracts them, makes them smile and laugh, the minister's well-being will be quickly restored as they prepare to go back to work the following day.

Hiring new staff members is a challenging process. Every search I've been a part of has had unexpected twists and turns. A staff search is often a painstaking process, involving a lot of resume-reading, lengthy dialogue with discerning leaders, and sometimes traveling to see the prospective staff member in their natural habitat. Searches can be interpersonally painful, because for every person you hire you will likely tell many, many worthy candidates that they are 'not the right fit' for the job. But when you see a new staff member gel with your team and be embraced by your church and help you further your mission, the pain is greatly rewarded.

RESPONSE TO: THE ENVELOPE

By: Andy McQuitty

Larry's nine criteria for new staff hires are laden with the wisdom of (much painful) experience and that's what makes them absolutely invaluable!

The most gut-wrenching thing I had to as a senior pastor was an occasional staff-firing. I quickly learned that the hard work of hiring right was way easier than enduring the grief of letting someone go. You'll definitely hire right if you follow Larry's criteria (which I'm not sure I myself could have met, so it's a good thing I never applied to work for my good friend)!

Allow me to supplement Larry's new staff criteria with two practical steps that we developed for the on-boarding process.

1. Follow this consistent and repeatable process for hiring:

    *   -Pray.
    *   Work up a description of the job including roles, authority, responsibility, character, skills, credentials, experience etc. The Department Head, who is responsible for the new hire, supervises this entire process (Children's Pastor for Children's ministry, Sr/Exec Pastor for staff pastors, etc.)
    *   Get the word out to see who might surface.
    *   Filter through all that.
    *   Narrow it down to a few quality candidates for an initial interview.(This is where we are looking for Larry's criteria above!)

- Usually, one sticks out.
- For that one, we check ten references: (2) they have worked for, (2) they have worked with, (2) that have worked for them, (2) mentors, (2) friends.

2. We **second interview** them (see Step 2 below). In the case of a Pastoral level position (Senior Ministry Team), representatives of the elder board will participate. Questions gleaned from their ten references are discussed.

3. For the third and decisive interview, we put together a group of random staff that interviews the candidate to see if we have missed any issue and to see if they will "fit" into our overall team. They may have talent, heart, experience, and skill but they may not fit into the IBC staff culture. Depending on the position and the role we sometimes pull into this some key lay people to help us make this decision. If it is a ministry leader (pastor/director) we ask that an elder be a part of this team interview as well.

  - Following the third interview we make an up or down call and then move forward.

4. Get the prospective staff member's responses and comments to our staff culture goals as defined below in the IBC Staff Handbook (written by IBC's executive team).

Going over these goals with a prospective staff member in the context of the second job interview is a great benefit to them. The process is not just informative about our church's staff values, but actually formative as it inspires new staffers to strive personally for a healthy staff culture from day one. Here are a couple of examples:

1. We Honor One Another

   How am I demonstrating that I value others?

We use our words and actions to support and encourage our coworkers. We refuse to engage in gossip or suspicion. Instead, we choose to believe the best about one another. We navigate conflict humbly and directly and do our best to embody Jesus' example of grace and truth. We respect one another's time, talents, and opinions. We pray for our church and one another.

2. We Bless One Another

How can I joyfully pitch in?

We collaborate and support one another across departments and teams. We look for ways to serve and care for one another and their families.

3. We Go For Great

How am I doing my work with excellence to honor God?

We believe our work reflects God; therefore, we pursue excellence and take godly pride in all we do. We honor our commitments and deadlines. We are careful to keep our work from becoming an idol we worship or something that defines us. We take the initiative to make IBC and our city a better place.

4. We Pursue the Same Vision

How can I help us move forward as a unified team?

We own and embrace that we are members of one body striving toward one vision. We remain open-handed with our plans and preferences so that we can remain unified in pursuit of this one vision.

5. We Grow

What practical steps am I taking to develop my personal, professional and spiritual life?

We take responsibility for our own growth and development, making our relationship with Jesus our first and highest priority. We seek out opportunities to learn, to risk, and to be challenged. We value diverse perspectives and wise counsel.

6. We Have Fun

How can I bring joy and laughter to my staff family?

Kingdom people are celebratory people; therefore, we set a joyful example in the healthy and hearty enjoyment of God's good gifts and the good work he has called us to do. We do not take ourselves too seriously.

9

SLOTH IS FOR SLOTHS

By Andy McQuitty

Okay, I'm going to say it out loud (and then write it down!). "We ministry leaders need to get serious about battling sloth!" Full disclosure—for four decades, I found this vice to be one of the most insidious enemies of my pastoral soul.

Now settle down, I'm not referring to the concept of sloth that most now hold—that of a good-for-nothing lazy shirker whose favorite hymn is "Nearer My Couch to Thee". Though most people today understand sloth to be physical laziness, in the original seven deadly sins as defined by theologians in the Middle Ages, sloth was 'sadness.' The original word for sloth, *acedia* (from the Greek *akedia*, "not to care"), meant spiritual listlessness, an apathetic indifference to the things God cares about, and the resulting shirking of our spiritual duty to him. *Acedia* was considered sinful because listless inaction (in both the spiritual and worldly realms) was considered just as sinful as wrong actions.

So yes, sloth does include being a couch potato, but it also (and more importantly for pastors) means allowing ourselves to be "overcome by adversity" (as the Anglican prayer book puts it) to the point that the resulting sadness makes us give up, grow complacent, or become resigned to living a spiritually apathetic life.

Lord knows we pastors have disheartening adversity in spades in the ministry—recalcitrant Boards, dogged fatigue, ungrateful church members, hollowed out bank accounts, harsh critics, diminished family time, political schisms in the congregation, difficult sermons, emotional Emergency Room all-nighters, disunified leadership, and … I'm just getting started!

See what I just did there? I offered perfectly good reasons (not excuses!) for pastors (especially like myself) to slide into sloth which is exactly what the Devil wants and exactly what we under-shepherds of Christ must reject. Os Guinness tells us why:

"Sloth is far more than indolence, physical laziness, or a state of couch-potato lethargy. It is a condition of explicitly spiritual dejection that has given up on the pursuit of God, the true, the good, and the beautiful"[7]

In my experience, the spiritual dejection that occasionally tempts me (and possibly you?) to give up on the pursuit of the true, good, and beautiful has two basic sources. The first one is personal failure. When I say personal failure, I'm not talking about "the big stuff" here— huge moral, potentially career-ending imbroglios or misdeeds. "The

---

7 Os Guiness and Virginia Moody, _Steering Through Chaos: Vice and Virtue in an Age of Moral Confusion_ (NavPress: July 5, 2000), p. 149

big stuff" might actually be easier to confront and conquer because they're public and undeniable. The personal failure I'm talking about is the million little failures that, largely hidden from the world, nibble us into *acedia* with guilt and self-shaming.

Examples of these insidious little failures are:

- Selfishly nursing bitterness from an old wound
- Eruptions of temper/pride/biting sarcasm
- Self-pity ("I'm so misunderstood")
- Bouts of laziness (not *acedia*, but avoiding doing the hard thing and covering it up by doing a whole bunch of "Type A" easy things instead!)

These examples of niggling little failures may or may not be straight out of my own life, but I'll never tell!

Is it possible that some of you have done the same? You have let our Lord down by running when you should have stood, or caving in when you should have resisted, or staying passive when you should have acted? If so, welcome to the sloth party where miserable guilt leads us to punish ourselves by intentionally placing ourselves beyond the reach of God's mercy. There we eventually wake up and realize that we've allowed *Acedia* to strangle our souls.

I hate that kind of waking up for many reasons, the main one being that the strangulation was not necessary! At the risk of over-simplifying, may I remind us pastors that a repentant heart and a willingness to come back are all God requires for our forgiveness. As Martin Luther famously discovered from the Book of Romans, no crawling on your knees, no acts of penance, no periods of detention are required for the forgiveness even of the sins of the clergy! What we preach about God's grace and forgiveness applies to us just as much (even more, possibly?) to ourselves!

Forgiveness is a function of God's grace, and grace is free even to pastors who simply trust God to forgive us according to His word and get us back into the game without unnecessary fuss or muss.

A second major source of sloth for me is trekking through the occasional spiritual desert. "Desert" is a metaphor for those spiritually thirsty seasons in our lives when we're discouraged or struggling and when, despite our best efforts to connect with God in prayer, it seems like our requests just bounce off the ceiling. We study God's word, but it seems archaic and irrelevant. We preach our hearts out, but folks keep checking their watches because it's a 12 p.m. kickoff for the Cowboys so PLEASE finish early!

In the desert, we still love God, but we're troubled because we can't understand Him or figure out where He is or if He still cares. Sometimes we spring bright-eyed out of bed and say, "Good morning, God." But in the desert, we pry open our eyelids and dejectedly say, "Good God, it's morning." In the desert, we still believe in God but wonder sometimes if He still believes in us. King David knew this desert. And thankfully, he knew the way out of it as shown in Psalm 42:1: "As the deer pants for streams of water, so my soul pants for you, O God. 2 My soul thirsts for God, for the living God"

Even in the desert, David prays. You say, "But how can I pray to someone who seems absent?" Consider this: God's silence should never be misconstrued as God's absence. As Israel learned in their desert, God may be silent, but He is nonetheless relentlessly faithful to His people:

"The LORD your God has blessed you in all the work of your hands. He has watched over your journey through this vast desert. These forty years the LORD your God has been with you, and you have not lacked anything" (Dt. 2.7).

In other words, even in the desert, God provides good things for His people. That's where He purged the children of Israel of unbelief. That's where He directed Elijah to the discovery of Elisha. That's where Jesus demonstrated his power over the evil one and his tempting ways. I conclude that some of the most important things in life are best learned in a barren desert where God's abundant provision is best seen. That may be a hard reality. But my brother pastors, I submit it's also a blessed one.

I believe Martin Luther would agree with me! I alluded earlier to the fact that "The Father of the Protestant Reformation" was subject throughout his life to bouts of depression, self-doubt, and despair. *Acedia*, in other words! Outwardly cheerful and devout, inside Martin Luther was often in crisis—tormented by feelings of his own unworthiness. But then this man publicly committed himself to the way of faith and forgiveness in 1517 by hammering his famous 95 theses to the Wittenberg Cathedral Church door.

We all know that act of nailing was theologically and historically significant! But it was personally significant as well. When Martin hammered that paper to the door, He said "no" to sloth, boldly refusing to entertain the possibility of giving up on the pursuit of God, the true, the good, and the beautiful.

Brothers, sloth is for sloths. So keep your hammers handy!

RESPONSE TO: THE DESERT

By Larry Parsley

I had a complicated reaction to this fine essay. That's understating it: I was deeply conflicted by it. My first reaction was an irrational fear that Andy had gotten his hand on a secret trove of my worst mental transcripts as a pastor. I felt exposed by the description of *acedia* in all its pastoral manifestations.

My second reaction (after I calmed down) was "thank God" (literally) "that Andy is talking about this." *Someone needs to talk about this!* We need the contribution of Os Guinness' elegant phrase "explicitly spiritual dejection" in our pastoral vocabulary. We need it especially when we find ourselves with Elijah in the desert of fatigue and self-pity, when 'the journey is too much" for us (1 Kings 19:7). Andy and I both encourage pastors to consider lengthy tenures, but one of the challenges of a long stay is you can begin to feel like you drag the accumulated trailer of your professional failures behind you. When this happens, our forward progress slows to a truly sloth-like pace.

I was so glad that Martin Luther figured so prominently in this chapter. In his slim, potent volume on Luther's <u>Heidelberg Disputation</u> (*On Being a Theologian of the Cross*), Gerhard Forde speaks of the "glory story." Forde says that in the glory story, we blindly proclaim that we "came from glory and are bound for glory" and nothing is going to stop our forward progress as Christians. Even if we are temporarily derailed from time to time, the "glory story" narrative assures us all we need is to fix ourselves is some "proper religious effort" and we'll be back on the "glory road" in no time. Luther was not a fan of the glory story; he called instead for "theologians of the cross," theologians who speak honestly about our pain and suffering and our inability to even *find* the "glory road" of life, much less *follow* it.

Too many of us pastors launch our careers with a 'glory story' — *I'm going to build a great church, and perhaps parley that into transferring to an even greater church* (all for the glory of God, you understand). God is gracious to let such dreams falter. But in the faltering, in the failure, in the utter and explicit spiritual dejection, we cry out to the one who prayed Psalm 22 from the cross. This is where our salvation lies.

10

WHAT THE PASTOR NEEDS MOST

SIGN: THE PLAN

By Larry Parsley

Many years ago, a pastor friend was going on a summer sabbatical, and he invited several of his friends to preach for him while he was away. He emailed all of us and said the summer series would be entitled, "What the Church Needs Now is _____." As fill-in preachers, our job was to preach a sermon on a suggested fill in the blank. The topics would be assembled on a 'first come, first served' basis. As soon as I saw the email, I knew I needed to act fast before all the 'good topics' were taken and I would be left with "what the church needs now is <u>puppet ministry</u>" or some such. I immediately fired back an email with the first word that came to mind: "What the Church Needs Now ..." I wrote, "is...Humility."

I passed over all nine Fruit of the Spirit, as well as what were then trendy topics like "leadership" or "relevance." Still, I've begun to wonder if that word that popped into my head was somehow the barely visible part of an iceberg in my soul. I've begun to wonder if humility is not only what the church needs, and not just now, but also what the pastorate needs, now more than ever.

WHY HUMILITY?

Humility is something we pastors know we need more of—much more. We would have to be blind to miss how many times in the Bible we are warned of humility's arch-nemesis: pride. Pride precedes destruction (Proverbs 16:18), after all. Pride is the opposite of love (1 Corinthians 13:4). So yes, we could almost see humility as a defense strategy or insurance policy against the costly damage pride can cause.

But is humility one of those chores that simply must be done, despite how much we abhor it? Is it like cleaning the gutters or decluttering the garage? I don't think so. A cursory glance at a concordance suggests that humility is a gateway to spiritual treasure. It gives access to God's favor (Proverbs 3:34) and guidance (Psalm 25:9) and wisdom (Proverbs 11:2). Pride eventually proves the law of spiritual gravity—those who vainly launches themselves upward must eventually come down. But humility defies the normal human gravitational pull. The Lord Himself promises to exalt the humble (Matthew 23:12).

But Pastor, you knew all of that before you started reading this chapter.

And yes, the weight of Scripture should provide ample motivation! Still, I think humility is frequently misunderstood and left untried. We learn the rhetorical tricks of sounding humble (something of a vocational necessity), while pride serves as a secret navigational system in our thoughts and passions.

So why this plea for pastoral humility?

Yes, it is a virtue, and Christians (especially leaders) should choose virtue over vide. Still, I think more is at play. What if humility is a secret, or a superpower, or a fundamental way God has wired His world? What if humility lays down the track on which the Kingdom of God runs?

I write as someone who has an uneasy relationship with humility. I know her counterfeits well, whether it is uncertainty or passivity or cowardice. I also know pride on an intimate basis. I cannot count the number of times that a silent "who do you think you are?" or "do you realize who I am?" has arisen in my soul. Every now and then, while searching for some note in a long-ago email, I come across a missive I actually sent out into the world, and I am appalled at how pompous and caustic it is.

At the same time, I aspire to humility and have seen just enough of it in others (and at times my own life) to testify to its longevity and strength. Allow me to make my case.

1. HUMILITY IS A STRATEGY.

For the pastor as well as for the lay Christian, humility is strategic. It offers a vote of, if not *no confidence*, then small confidence in one's own ability to fathom life's mysteries. Because of that, it trusts scripture over instinct and God over self.

Humility consistently says, '*I don't think I have the whole picture here. I don't believe my first instinct is necessarily the best one. There's so much more I could learn before I act.*' In this sense, humility leads a pastor to have a greater hunger for available wisdom than the pastor's mind currently possesses.

This strategy opposes the notion that we are supposed to always know how to lead and where to lead and what to say. It dares to pray and to ask God and the wise people God has loaned to us: "What do you think?"

2. HUMILITY IS A VANTAGE POINT.

John the Baptist would make a strange role model for a pastor. Everything from his diet to his wardrobe to his isolation and especially his biting sermon applications would make him the least likely pastor to celebrate a 5-year anniversary.

And yet, could we pastors find a better role model when it comes to John's humble relationship with Jesus? For those of us who frequently feel like others fail to grant us enough respect, John offers a bracing contrast. He continually told others what he was NOT. He preferred to be simply a wilderness voice pointing away from himself and towards the 'Lamb of God who takes away the sins of the world.'

Similarly, humility is a vantage point by which to observe Jesus. It is hard to see Jesus through the windshield when we're fixing our hair in the mirror. Humility helps us stand, like the best man in the wedding, in the perfect vantage point to see Jesus profess His love to His bride, the church. There is a fullness of joy that is possible when we would rather be the Best Man than step between the church and her beloved.

3. HUMILITY IS A PROMISE.

It is common to speak of pastors in my station of life as being in the "fourth quarter" of ministry. In my case, that is generous (I'm likely nearer the two-minute warning than I'd like to admit). Regardless of the metaphor, there is a sense where the life of the pastor is a contest, ideally played over four-plus decades. Some years, pastors will feel like they are losing. Yet, when we take the long view, we will see the promise of Matthew 23:12, that those "who exalt themselves will be humbled, and those who humble themselves will be exalted."

One of the advantages of seeing the game from the viewpoint of the fourth quarter is the insight it has given me on pastors I once envied. Over the last three quarters, I've watched pastoral thought leaders drift uncomfortably far from orthodoxy; some have succumbed to sexual temptation and indeed been guilty of sexual abuse; some have been credibly accused of a bullying behavior that is wholly incompatible with those handed a shepherd's crook. I say this not to gloat over their failure, but rather to confess my pride. I once coveted the 'exaltation' of their earthly platforms. I bought their books and sometimes copied their formulas.

Today, I realize my envy of them was laced with pride. And all the while, James 3:13 was hiding in plain sight in my Bible: "Who is wise and understanding among you? Let them show it by their good life, by deeds done in the humility that comes from wisdom." Humility offers the promise of a wise way of living the life of the pastor. It teaches a life of unspectacular words and deeds that, over the long haul, reveal a pastoral version of the "good life."

I said it then and I'll say it again: what the church needs now, and surely what the pastorate needs now, is humility.

RESPONSE TO: THE PLAN

By: Andy McQuitty

With these 4 sentences, my wise colleague has completely changed my perspective on the virtue of humility:

"But is humility one of those chores that simply must be done, despite how much we abhor it? Is it like cleaning the gutters or decluttering the garage? I don't think so. A cursory glance at a concordance suggests that humility is a gateway to spiritual treasure."

You nailed me, Larry! Yes, I have always taken the "gutter cleaning" view of humility as the necessary chore of slapping-down pride which we all know is death-in-the-pot to spiritual leadership. And I've joked about "praying for humility" as being a dangerous request of God because He just might grant it by painfully destroying our pride. But of course, we should do it anyway because, though difficult and often unpleasant, it's a necessary discipline (chore!) for our sanctification as pastors!

And yes, I've preached on Jesus' rebuke of His disciples' prideful, intramural "race to the top" in Mark 9:33-37 as he takes a little child in his arms who cannot give things but only needs things and must have things done for her and essentially says: "Here's your ministry. Be humble. Give yourselves to those who can bring you no status or clout. You need to help this little child, not just for her sake, but more for your sake. For if you don't, your whole life will be thrown away on an idiotic contest to see who's the greatest."

That's all fine and good, but my deficiency in the conversation about the need to fight pride has been conflating humility with pride's destruction. Surely the two are related in that humility does come when pride goes. But the two are not the same. Pride is a vice. Humility is a virtue. We fight our vices as enemies to our souls, but we cultivate our virtues as treasures in our spiritual storehouses. Pride is a threat to our spiritual health which we must grimly battle. But as my astute friend wrote, "…*humility is a gateway to spiritual treasure*" which we must joyfully pursue!

Thanks Larry for helping me do just that by seeing humility as an independent virtue (like wisdom) to be cultivated for a lifetime, and not just a weapon against pride. That virtue-cultivation becomes doable as we see humility for what Larry insightfully defines it to be—a *strategy* (for having a greater hunger for available wisdom than the pastor's mind currently possesses), a *vantage point* (by which to observe Jesus), and a *promise* (that those "who exalt themselves will be humbled, and those who humble themselves will be exalted").

This perspective on humility (which is similar to what Tim Keller defines as the "Christian Gospel") actually motivates me to pursue humility (instead of dreading its arrival!) and believe that I can actually grow the virtue of humility in my life as I cultivate it. As Keller says:

"The Christian Gospel is that I am so flawed that Jesus had to die for me, yet I am so loved and valued that Jesus was glad to die for me. This leads to deep humility and deep confidence at the same time. It undermines both swaggering and sniveling. I cannot feel superior to anyone, and yet I have nothing to prove to anyone. I do not think more of myself nor less of myself. Instead, I think of myself less"[8]

---

[8] *(Timothy Keller, The Reason for God: Belief in an Age of Skepticism).*

Please excuse me now because I have gutters to clean and a garage to declutter!

11

HOW TO HANG IN THERE

SIGN: THE TREK

By Andy McQuitty

The average church tenure for a senior pastor in America today is 5–7 years. But if you include all pastoral positions, that number falls to 3–4 years.[9] I'm not denying that there are valid reasons for short pastorates. There are! But still I am troubled by the question: why do so many, leave so soon?

I have come to believe it's because many pastors enter the ministry without a clear understanding of the difficulties they will inevitably face and therefore the advance decisions they must definitively take if they are to survive and thrive in their pastorates.

Let me explain by telling the following true story (that I'm also using metaphorically of the ministry!) about a professor at a Christian college who decided to go with his son on a 1,000-mile backpacking

---

9 (Lifeway, Oct 13, 2021).

trip from British Columbia to southern California. Before leaving on the trip, the professor discovered that over 90% of those who set out to hike more than 500 miles never made it. 50% never even get started, and 40% quit after they start. *Only 10% ever finish a long-distance hike.*

After studying the 10%, the professor discovered that, before their trip, those who succeeded made two important decisions: First, they decided *they would finish the trip no matter what happened.* Second, *they expected bad things to happen and decided they would not be surprised or dismayed.* Having taken these two essential advance decisions for themselves, the professor and his son set out on their journey through the mountains of Washington, Oregon, and California.

For many days they were alone on the trail, often camping above the 10,000-foot level. They faced every sort of discouragement: lack of food and water, danger from wild animals, danger from robbers they might meet, days of rain and mud, incredible physical exhaustion, the very real possibility of physical injury, not to speak of loneliness, blisters, mosquitoes, and the extremes of heat and cold. But when the rains turned the trail into a quagmire, they didn't quit because they had decided *they would finish the trip no matter what happened* and weren't surprised or dismayed. When black clouds of mosquitoes descended like an Old Testament plague, they didn't quit because they weren't surprised or dismayed. When they faced days of loneliness and nights of hunger, they didn't quit because they *knew* it would be like this. They weren't surprised or dismayed. And as a result, they completed their 1,000-mile trip in record time.

I believe we pastors need to accept our calls to church ministry (our "1,000-mile trip") with the same mindset. We must purpose from the start to finish the trip and not be surprised or dismayed by adversity. We need to refuse to quit and just keep putting one foot in front of the other. Yes, we'll take a step and hit the mud (contrarians who resist change and progress). Yes, we'll take another step and confront a bear (a board member who has it in for us). Yes, we'll take another step and our legs begin to cramp (the relentless weariness of weekly preaching and staff meetings and money problems). Yes, we'll take another step and the crazy people come out of the woods (implacable critics set on sabotaging our ministry). Doesn't matter. We won't be surprised because we knew the insurmountable problems and crazy people would show up sooner or later! We set out to finish well despite expected "loneliness, blisters, and black clouds of mosquitoes". Just like the Apostle Paul did:

"But in all things approving ourselves as the ministers of God, in much patience, in afflictions, in necessities, in distresses, in stripes, in imprisonments, in tumults, in labours, in watchings, in fastings." 2 Corinthians 6:4-5

Evidently, Paul had made our two crucial decisions before starting his "race". He had decided *he would finish the race* no matter what happened. Second, *he expected bad things to happen and decided he would not be surprised or dismayed.* Those bad things did happen, and yes, Paul did finish his race even though they did! Can you sense Paul's joy in this on the eve of his execution in Rome?

"I have fought the good fight, I have finished the race, I have kept the faith. Henceforth there is laid up for me the crown of righteousness, which the Lord, the righteous judge, will award to me on that day, and not only to me but also to all who have loved his appearing" (2 Timothy 4:7-8).

If you're like me, you might be tempted to chalk up Paul's triumphant resume of endurance to his extraordinary spiritual strength and discipline. That's a convenient conclusion because it lets me (and all other non-Paul-the-Apostles) off the hook for pursuing similar perseverance!

But no, in the end Paul's "fighting the good fight and finishing his race" was due, not to his superior courage and self-discipline, but to God's magnificent faithfulness and grace (which is available to us all!). As the great Eugene Peterson declares:

"For perseverance is not resignation, putting up with things the way they are, staying in the same old rut year after year, or being a doormat for people to wipe their feet on. Endurance is not a desperate hanging on but a traveling from strength to strength. . .The central reality for Christians is the personal, unalterable, persevering commitment God makes to us. Perseverance is not the result of our determination; it is the result of God's faithfulness. We survive in the way of faith not because we have extraordinary stamina but because God is righteous, because God sticks with us" (Eugene Peterson, A Long Obedience In The Same Direction, pp. 37-8)).

Friends, here's my hobo sign for this chapter: the most memorable and glorious and enjoyable hikes of our lives are also the hardest and most arduous and most demanding hikes of our lives (which we finish only because God sticks with us!).

RESPONSE TO: THE TREK

By: By Larry Parsley

Andy, this may be my favorite chapter in the book. I concur with your conviction that God is sovereign over a pastor's vocational journey. Accordingly, not every pastor will receive the "Pastoral Longevity Merit Badge." Still, I fear too many pastors leave their churches too soon, and in so doing miss out on the beauty of a fruitful long-term ministry.

Your illustration of the 1,000-mile hike is well-played. As we urge 22-year-olds in premarital counseling to envision the beauty of slicing into that 50th wedding anniversary cake one day, we should similarly encourage pastors to commit to staying with their current call until God releases them (likely not fifty years, but hopefully more than two!).

As someone blessed to spend almost 24 years pastoring in one church, I can testify to the 'mosquitos" that nag and the austere parts of the trail that trigger dreams of quitting. More importantly, I thank God for all those Monday mornings and Sunday afternoons when I did not give in to that temptation. If so, I would have never witnessed the beauty of marrying young adults whom I once dedicated as infants, baptized as children, and served alongside on youth mission trips. I would have missed seeing prodigals far from God return from the 'far county'. I would never have celebrated those brand-new ministerial staff members, green with inexperience, who one day flourish like palm trees in the courts of the Lord (Psalm 92:12).

I have been blessed by the 'compound interest' of a long-term pastorate, watching God's grace multiply through the years. And Andy, I have been cheered on knowing that you covered more terrain than me and kept on hiking. May your words - indeed, may the Holy Spirit - spur more and more of our readers to a 'long *pastoral* obedience in the same direction.' Amen.

12

THE NECESSITY OF PASTORAL FRIENDSHIP

SIGN: THE JERSEY

By Larry Parsley

Two basketball players move into the paint, their eyes elevated toward the orange sphere that bounces upward off the rim. At precisely the same moment, both leap, intent on securing the ball. A second later, four hands surround one ball. Both players are *competitors*; neither are about to let the other rip the ball from their hands. Suddenly, a familiar voice shouts in the direction of both players: "Same Team! SAME team!" The two players, it turns out, wear the same jersey. The problem arose when their circle of vision became so small that they could not see they were grappling with a teammate.

As a pastor living through an era of intense church competition, I have found that learning to view other pastors in our community as players on the *same team* is as difficult as it is necessary. One of the unfortunate byproducts of the business world's influence on churches in the late 20th and early 21st centuries is an obsessive sense of barely concealed competition between local churches. In our quest to gain market share of tithing church members, we can begin to see churches down the street as *opponents*. Our private rhetoric toward fellow pastors can become harsh, as we cast aspersions upon their ministry methods and complain that they are "stealing" our church members. I am not proud of the *schadenfreude* which arises in my heart whenever I hear of something negative happening at the fastest-growing churches in my area. Surely the Devil rejoices when supposed members of the same team fight with one another over supremacy. Such things must be continually confessed to God.

Along the way, as I have confessed jealousy and resentment, I have also encountered a potent antibiotic for church competition—namely, pursuing spiritual community with neighboring pastors. One of the best things your community's pastors can do is to invest time and effort into pastoral fellowship. If you are like me, the calls from *inside* the church will constantly dissuade you from making time for pastoral friendship *outside* the church. Nevertheless, I want you to consider for a moment what can happen when local pastors invest time and emotion into befriending one another.

Imagine the visual message a community witnesses when area pastors sit in harmony around the same lunch tables? The visual message is that these local clergy are not rivals but companions.

Imagine what happens when pastors, if only for a few minutes, read God's Word *together* and pray? Or when they help one another troubleshoot problems, and when they share resources?

What happens in a community when pastors participate in community-wide thanksgiving services or prayer services? When they loan one another facilities for funerals?

What spiritual medicines are released in a congregation that publicly intercedes for other churches in their community?

The message we pastors continually need to hear when our spiritual vision has contracted to our own congregational ambitions is this: "Same Team!" We wear the same Kingdom of God jerseys.

Allow me to share just a few blessings I've witnessed when pastors covenant to become friends and have the "same team" mindset.

1. **Curbs jealousy**: It is exceedingly difficult to resent the success of someone who has put their hand on my shoulder to pray for me about some challenge I'm walking through.

2. **Pools Wisdom**: Being on the same team can elucidate our understand our shared ministry context. What if neighboring pastors are facing the same cultural and civic challenges that you face? If so, it can help you not feel so alone.

3. **Curbs Church-hopping:** We live in an ecclesial season where church loyalty is abysmally low. People leave churches when worship feels stale, when favorite staff members leave, when feathers get ruffled, and when children feel like they don't know anyone in their Sunday School class. Most pastors I know share a common experience: You greet a guest in a church lobby after worship and you ask them if they are new to the community. "No," they respond, "we have actually lived here for 10 years." Then a frown covers their face as they begin to mention the neighboring church where they used to be members. And just as they are about to undercut that church or to criticize its

pastor, you preempt that criticism by saying something to the effect of, "Oh, I'm a big fan of that church; her pastor is a great friend of mine!" Nothing undercuts church competition like letting people know that we're on the *same team*.

Here is precisely where I need to affirm my co-author, Andy Mc-Quitty. Andy and I were "church neighbors" for over 20 years. During that time, his church's membership was larger, his staff was larger, his budget was larger, and his reach was larger than ours. On a merely human level, it would have been easy for me to envy Andy, and it would have been easy for Andy to ignore me. Instead, Andy welcomed me as a friend and partner. Whenever I would call him with a challenge I was facing, he would immediately suggest we meet right away for lunch at the barbecue place halfway between our two churches. Andy practiced open-source ministry, freely sharing his time and expertise, and I greedily absorbed so much from him. Over the course of our pastorates, I preached at his church, and he preached at mine. We both spoke to leaders at the other's churches. And today, Andy gives full-time effort to sharing this beautiful message of pastoral friendship through the ministry of Kaleo Collective. How thankful I am for a friend who literally practices what he preaches. How thankful I am to play with him on the same team!

RESPONSE TO: THE JERSEY

By Andy McQuitty

Larry writes, "I am not proud of the *schadenfreude* which arises in my heart whenever I hear of something negative happening at the fastest-growing churches in my area." I'm probably not proud of the *schadenfreude* in my heart either, but I'm not sure because, well, what on earth *is* that? (Once again my D.Min proves inferior to my buddy's Ph.D!).

Two things I do know: a great barbecue place is a powerful pastoral friendship builder (there's a prooftext for this in Proverbs somewhere I think), and I'm so thankful for the same-jersey friendship I've shared with Larry over these many years!" I'm thankful for it not just because it was a wonderful and rare serendipity. But also because I've come to see it was an absolute essential of survival!

In 2011, Lance Witt published the following stat's which I believe explain why hundreds of pastors in America leave the ministry each month and (tragically!) why only one of every ten current ministers will retire as a minister![10]

- 80% of pastors and 85% of their spouses feel discouraged in their roles.
- 70% of pastors do not have a close friend, confidant, or mentor (a 2021 Lifeway Research Survey found that 64% of pastors believe a need they must address is "relationships with other pastors").

---

[10] Lance Witt, *Replenish* (pp. 18-19). Baker Publishing Group. Kindle Edition. 6.1.2011

- Over 50% of pastors are so discouraged they would leave the ministry if they could but have no other way of making a living.
- Over 50% of pastors' wives feel that their husband entering ministry was the most destructive thing to ever happen to their families.
- 71% of pastors stated they were burned out, and they battle depression beyond fatigue on a weekly and even a daily basis.

I don't see a single stat in this dismal list of clerical discouragements that could not be substantially improved by genuine friendships with other pastors, do you? I know it worked for Larry and me over the years, and I know it's working in Kaleo Collective even as we are just getting our zoom-based pastoral cohorts up and running (www.kaleocollective.org).

But what do I mean by "it's working"? Christina Braudaway-Bauman facilitated a pastoral friendship cohort and wrote up the compelling dynamics that resulted:

"The lesson emerging . . . is that when clergy meet regularly. . .they find that trust develops, anxieties diminish, and challenges turn into occasions for learning. . .Pastors help one another stay connected to the joy of ministry. As they gather together, prayer fills the air, laughter shakes the room, competition flies away, confidence takes deeper root. . . . calmer and more generous pastoral spirits grow in the rich soil of real community. Once pastors experience the transforming power of this community, they can no longer imagine doing ministry without it." ("Peer Power: The Promise of Clergy Support Groups" by Christina Braudaway-Bauman, <u>The Christian Century</u>, January 2, 2012).

I can't imagine having done ministry without making friends of my "same-jersey" teammates either! So let me urge all my pastoral colleagues: don't be a Lone Ranger! Instead, don the team jersey and you'll lose the *schadenfreude (thank goodness!)* and start having some fun in ministry alongside a vital, encouraging community of your peers!

AUTHORS' BIOGRAPHIES

Dr. Eric Andrew McQuitty (Pastor Andy) earned his Th.M at Dallas Theological Seminary in 1987 and his D.Min in 1996. He served as Sr. Pastor at Irving Bible Church for 32 years and became Pastor Emeritus at his retirement in 2019. Andy married his wife, Alice, in 1978 and is Dad to 5 wonderful children and Pops to 6 absolutely exceptional grandchildren. Andy founded Kaleo Collective in 2022 to provide spiritual encouragement and advice on best leadership practices to pastors across the nation through ongoing Zoom communities of their peers. Andy has previously published three books: *Notes from the Valley: A Spiritual Travelogue through Cancer, The Way to Brave: Shaping a David Faith in Our Goliath World, and Your Best Life Later: What Every Daughter and Son Need to Know.*

Larry Parsley is a Clinical Professor of Christian Ministry and the Director of Mentoring for Baylor's Truett Seminary. He joined the faculty in the summer of 2023 after serving as senior pastor of Valley Ranch Baptist in Coppell (a suburb of Dallas) for over 23 years. He is a contributor and speaker for Mockingbird Ministries and writes for Christianity Today's *Preaching Today.*